Tributes
AND
Treasures

Tributes
AND
Treasures

12 Vintage-Inspired Quilts
Made with Reproduction Prints

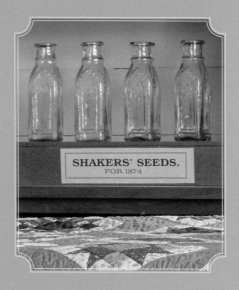

Paula Barnes AND Mary Ellen Robison
OF RED CRINOLINE QUILTS

Martingale®
Create with Confidence

Dedication

To John Robert "JR" Barnes
May 4, 1953—May 4, 2013
Loving husband and father, friend,
advisor, and loyal supporter

Tributes and Treasures: 12 Vintage-Inspired Quilts
Made with Reproduction Prints
© 2015 by Paula Barnes and Mary Ellen Robison

Martingale®
19021 120th Ave. NE, Ste. 102
Bothell, WA 98011-9511 USA
ShopMartingale.com

Printed in China
20 19 18 17 16 15   8 7 6 5 4 3 2 1

Library of Congress Cataloging-in-Publication Data is available upon request.

ISBN: 978-1-60468-567-1

Mission Statement

Dedicated to providing quality products
and service to inspire creativity.

Credits

PUBLISHER AND CHIEF VISIONARY OFFICER
Jennifer Erbe Keltner

EDITORIAL DIRECTOR
Karen Costello Soltys

DESIGN DIRECTOR
Paula Schlosser

MANAGING EDITOR
Tina Cook

STUDIO PHOTOGRAPHER
Brent Kane

ACQUISITIONS EDITOR
Karen M. Burns

LOCATION PHOTOGRAPHER
Adam Albright

TECHNICAL EDITOR
Ellen Pahl

PRODUCTION MANAGER
Regina Girard

COPY EDITOR
Melissa Bryan

ILLUSTRATOR
Christine Erikson

PHOTOGRAPH CREDITS

The vintage photographs in this book are in the public domain or used by permission.

"Plantation Road," page 34, from the collections of The Henry Ford.

"Crossroads," page 66, from the Library of Congress.

"Sallie's Quilt," page 72, by permission of Peter D. Robison.

"Oak Alley," page 80, image courtesy of Oak Alley Plantation, Vacherie, Louisiana.

SPECIAL THANKS

To the staff of The Garden Barn of Indianola, Iowa, and Living History Farms of Urbandale, Iowa, thank you for generously allowing us to take photographs on location. For more information, visit:

The Garden Barn: www.thegardenbarn.com
Living History Farms: www.lhf.org

CONTENTS

INTRODUCTION

"Write a book," they said. "You can do it," they said. And so we did! Just one more step as we continue along this journey we call Red Crinoline Quilts.

It all began around a kitchen table in Katy, Texas, in 2005. We were quilters, neighbors, and friends, and we had passion and a crazy idea—*let's open an online quilt store!* And now, almost 10 years later, our crazy idea has grown to become a quilt venture which allows us to travel throughout the United States, meet fellow quilters, and share our passion. We have endured numerous changes—growth, reorganization, new locations, and even a new name—but through it all, the passion remained and our friendship has grown.

As fellow quilters you understand—it's all about the fabric! Our love for 1800s reproduction prints and the quilts from that same era is always our focus. Paula is an avid collector of antique quilts and textiles that she uses as her inspiration for her quilt designs. In 2008, she expanded her talents into fabric design with Marcus Brothers Textiles. Now, many of our new quilts feature her fabric collections. Mary Ellen pieces all of our beautiful quilts. She is the lucky one who gets to actually play with the fabrics and take care of our many devoted customers. It's a partnership that works perfectly for us.

As our business grew, the number of quilt patterns we had designed increased. Many were featured in *American Patchwork and Quilting, Quiltmania, Primitive Quilts and Projects, McCall's,* and *Quilt* magazines. We also just introduced our fourth block-of-the-month program with Marcus Brothers Textiles. A book seemed to be the logical next step so we selected 12 of our favorite quilts to include. We hope you enjoy the much-loved quilts we're sharing in this book, and we look forward to continuing along this Red Crinoline Quilts journey with you.

Tavern Blues

On July 7, 1865, Mary Surratt became the first woman to be executed by the United States Government. Mary Elizabeth Jenkins married John Harrison Surratt at the age of seventeen. Mary's life with John was a hard one; her husband was an alcoholic and at times he was both physically and mentally abusive to Mary. In 1851, John built a new home and tavern in Clinton, Maryland. Surratt Tavern was a post office, a safe house for the Confederate underground, a polling place, and an inn before Mary was forced to rent it to an ex-policeman, John Lloyd. Mary and her three children moved into a townhouse, which she then opened as a boarding house. It was in this boarding house that Mary's son, John Surratt Jr., introduced her to John Wilkes Booth and the other conspirators in the plot to assassinate President Abraham Lincoln. It was the testimony of John Lloyd and Louis Weichmann, a resident of the boarding house, that proved crucial in the guilty verdict for Mary's role in the conspiracy. Her son, John Jr., was found innocent.

Mary Surratt

FINISHED QUILT: 94½" x 94½" ✳ FINISHED BLOCK: 12" x 12"
"Tavern Blues," designed by Paula Barnes, pieced by Mary Ellen Robison,
and machine quilted by Cathy Peters and Lynn Graham

Materials

Yardage is based on 42"-wide fabric.

3 yards of border print or stripe for outer border

2⅛ yards of tan stripe for sashing*

2 yards of blue print for setting triangles

1 yard of brown print for cornerstones and binding

½ yard *each* of 13 assorted dark-blue or brown
   prints for blocks

½ yard *each* of 6 assorted light prints for blocks

½ yard of light print for inner border

8¾ yards of fabric for backing

102" x 102" piece of batting

*If you use a print that you don't need to fussy cut, 1⅝ yards
is enough.*

Cutting

From *each* of the 6 assorted light prints, cut:
   7 strips, 2" x 42"; crosscut into 140 squares, 2" x 2"

From *each* of the 13 assorted dark prints, cut:
   3 strips, 3½" x 42"; crosscut into:
      18 squares, 3½" x 3½"
      24 rectangles, 2" x 3½"
   1 strip, 2" x 42"; crosscut into 8 squares, 2" x 2"

From the tan stripe, *fussy cut:**
   64 rectangles, 2½" x 12½"

From the brown print, cut:
   3 strips, 2½" x 42"; crosscut into 40 squares,
      2½" x 2½"
   10 strips, 1⅞" x 42"

*For a nondirectional print, cut 4 strips, 12½" x 42", and
crosscut the 64 sashing rectangles.*

From the blue print, cut:
  3 squares, 21⅛" x 21⅛"; cut into quarters
    diagonally to make 12 triangles
  2 squares, 12¼" x 12¼"; cut in half diagonally to
    make 4 triangles
From the light print for inner border, cut:
  9 strips, 1½" x 42"
From the border print, cut on the *lengthwise* grain:
  4 strips, 5½" x 99"

Making the Blocks

The cutting instructions yield enough pieces to make 26 blocks, two from each dark print. You'll need only 25 blocks for the quilt; make the additional block if desired, or add the pieces to your scraps. You'll have a few extra pieces left over even if you make the extra block. The blocks are made with two types of units: flying geese and square in a square.

1 Using a pencil or fabric marker, draw a straight line from corner to corner on the wrong side of 16 assorted light 2" squares.

2 Select eight matching dark 2" x 3½" rectangles. With right sides together, place a marked light square on one end of a dark rectangle, aligning the raw edges. Sew on the line and trim, leaving a ¼" seam allowance. Press the seam allowances toward the light print. Repeat with a second light square on the other end of the rectangle to make a flying-geese unit. Make eight flying-geese units using the same dark print.

Make 8.

3 Sew two flying-geese units and one matching dark 2" x 3½" rectangle together to create a star-point unit. Press the seam allowances toward the rectangle. Make four star-point units.

Make 4.

4 Using a pencil or fabric marker, draw a straight line from corner to corner on the wrong side of 16 assorted light 2" squares.

5 Select four matching dark 3½" squares; these can be from the same dark print used in the star-point units, or different if you prefer. In the quilt shown, some are the same and some are different. Mix and match prints as desired. With right sides together, place a marked light square on a dark 3½" square. Sew on the line and trim, leaving a ¼" seam allowance. Press the seam allowances toward the light print. Repeat to add a marked light square on the diagonally opposite corner. Repeat on the remaining corners. Make four square-in-a-square units using the same dark print.

Make 4.

6 Select five dark 3½" squares; these can be from the same dark print used in the flying-geese units, the square-in-a-square units, or different. Arrange the squares and the four units from step 5 in three rows as shown. Sew together in rows; press all seam allowances toward the unpieced squares. Sew the rows together to create the center of the block. Press seam allowances toward the top and bottom rows.

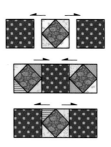 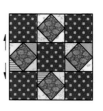

7 Select four dark 2" squares that match the flying-geese units. Sew the block center, the four star-point units, and the squares into three rows as

shown. Press the seam allowances as indicated by the arrows. Sew the rows together and press.

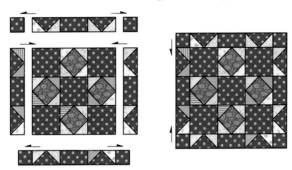

8 Repeat steps 1–7 to make a total of 25 blocks.

Constructing the Quilt

After completing the center of the quilt, always measure the length and width before cutting borders. Refer to "Measuring for Borders" on page 93.

1 Lay out the blocks, tan-striped sashing rectangles, and brown 2½" cornerstones in an on-point setting, with four blocks across and four blocks down. Rearrange until you are pleased with the color placement.

2 Sew the cornerstones and sashing rectangles together to create the sashing rows as indicated in the assembly diagram. Press the seam allowances toward the sashing rectangles and place the strips back in the layout.

3 Sew the pieced blocks and sashing rectangles together to create rows. Press the seam allowances toward the sashing. Place the block rows back in the layout.

4 Sew a sashing row and a block row together. Press the seam allowances toward the sashing and then add a side setting triangle to each end of the row. Repeat until all of the side setting triangles have been joined.

5 Sew the rows together. Press the seam allowances toward the sashing rows.

6 Add the corner triangles and press the seam allowances toward the triangles.

7 For the inner border, trim the selvages from the light 1½" x 42" strips and sew the strips together end to end. Press the seam allowances to one side. From

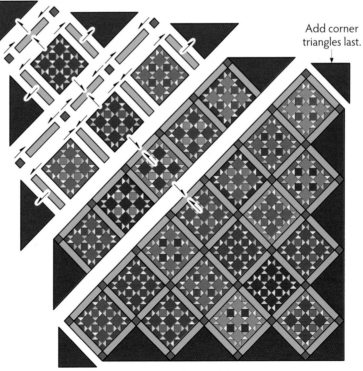

Add corner triangles last.

Quilt assembly

this strip cut two strips, 82½" long, for the side borders and two strips, 84½" long, for the top and bottom borders. Attach the side borders first, press the seam allowances toward the border strips, and then add the top and bottom borders. Press.

8 Referring to "Mitered Borders" on page 91, add the border-print strips to all four sides of the quilt and miter the corners. Press.

Finishing the Quilt

1 Layer the quilt top with the batting and backing. Quilt by hand or machine. The featured quilt was machine quilted to highlight the elements of the design, including a central circular feather motif and crosshatching on each block, feathers in the setting triangles and sashing, and parallel lines in the outer border.

2 Add binding using the 1⅞"-wide strips. If you need additional details, go to ShopMartingale.com for free downloadable information.

Adding borders

Hill Country Baskets

To induce settlers, the Republic of Texas issued colonization land grants for over four million acres of land to individuals with the stipulation that settlements be made in specific geographical areas and within a limited time period. The Fisher-Miller Land Grant was one of these grants and its intention was to bring 1,000 immigrants of German, Dutch, Swiss, Danish, Swedish, and Norwegian ancestry to the Texas Hill Country region.

Baron Otto von Meusebach of Germany was one of these settlers. Drawn to Texas by his love of geology, botany, and horticulture, the Baron dropped his German title of nobility and became John O. Meusebach. He arrived in Galveston on May 1, 1845, with the intention of assisting in the management and settlement of the land grant that had established New Braunfels and the surrounding area. Raids by the Comanche Indians were preventing the settlement of these areas, so he negotiated a treaty that gave the Comanches $3,000 in gifts, but gave the settlers so much more—the rights to safely settle on Comanche land. The Meusebach-Comanche Treaty signed on May 9, 1847, is considered to be one of the most important pioneer works for that time. Meusebach went on to found Fredericksburg, Castell, and Leiningen in the Hill Country.

The Texas Hill Country area was settled by large numbers of German immigrants who were supporters of the European revolution of 1848. In keeping with the ideals that led them to leave Germany, most of these "Forty-Eighters," as they became known, sided with the Union and served in the Union Army during the Civil War. The German population made up the majority of those who were against Texas seceding from the Union.

John Meusebach, founder of Fredericksburg, Texas

"Hill Country Baskets," designed by Paula Barnes, pieced by Mary Ellen Robison,
and machine quilted by Sharon Dixon

Materials

Yardage is based on 42"-wide fabric.

3 yards of dark-red print for outer border

2½ yards of light stripe for sashing*

1 yard of brown print for cornerstones and inner border

1 yard of medium-red print for setting triangles

*If you use a print that doesn't need to be fussy cut, 1⅝ yards is enough.

1 fat quarter *each* of 17 assorted light prints for blocks (basket)

1 fat quarter *each* of 17 assorted dark prints** for blocks (background)

⅛ yard *each* of 17 assorted medium prints** for blocks (basket center)

1 yard of fabric for binding

9 yards of fabric for backing

104" x 104" piece of batting

**These prints can range from medium to dark; to avoid confusion in the instructions, they'll be referred to as darks for the backgrounds and mediums for the basket centers.

Cutting

Do not cut the lengthwise border strips from the dark-red print until the quilt center is complete and you have determined the final measurements.

From *each* of the 17 assorted light prints, cut:
    10 rectangles, 2" x 3½"
    10 squares, 2¾" x 2¾"

From *each* of the 17 assorted dark prints, cut:
    10 rectangles, 2" x 3½"
    20 squares, 2" x 2"
    10 squares, 2¾" x 2¾"

From *each* of the 17 assorted medium prints, cut:
    10 squares, 2" x 2"

From the light stripe, *fussy cut*:
    196 rectangles, 2" x 6½"

From the brown print, cut:
    14 strips, 2" x 42"; crosscut 6 of the strips into
        112 squares, 2" x 2"

From the medium-red print, cut:
    6 squares, 11⅞" x 11⅞"; cut into quarters
        diagonally to make 24 triangles
    2 squares, 7¼" x 7¼"; cut in half diagonally to
        make 4 triangles

From the dark-red print, cut on the
    ***lengthwise* grain:**
    2 strips, 8½" x 80"
    2 strips, 8½" x 96"

From the binding fabric, cut:
    10 strips, 1⅞" x 42", or bias strips to total 400"

Making the Blocks

For each block, choose one light print, one dark print, and one medium print in the following sizes:

- **Light print for basket:** 2 rectangles, 2" x 3½", and 2 squares, 2¾" x 2¾"
- **Dark print for background:** 2 rectangles, 2" x 3½"; 4 squares, 2" x 2"; and 2 squares, 2¾" x 2¾"
- **Medium print for basket center:** 2 squares, 2" x 2"

1 Referring to "Half-Square-Triangle Units" on page 91, mark the light 2¾" squares and layer them right sides together with the dark 2¾" squares. Sew, cut, and trim to 2" x 2". Make four units, pressing seam allowances toward the light print in three units and toward the dark print in the remaining unit.

Make 4.

2 Using a pencil or fabric marker, draw a line diagonally from corner to corner on the wrong side of the two dark 2" squares.

3 Place a marked square right sides together on one end of a light 2" x 3½" rectangle and sew on the drawn line. Trim ¼" from the line and press the seam allowances toward the dark print. Repeat to make a second unit with the angle going in the opposite direction.

4 Sew a dark 2" x 3½" rectangle and a unit from step 3 together. Press seam allowances toward the dark rectangle. Make a second unit as shown.

Make 1 of each.

5 Sew two half-square-triangle units (pressed toward the light), one medium 2" square, and one dark 2" square together as shown. Press seam allowances as indicated.

Make 1.

6 Sew the remaining two half-square-triangle units, one medium 2" square, and one dark 2" square together as shown. Press seam allowances as indicated.

Make 1.

7 Sew the four pieced units together to make the block. Press seam allowances as indicated. The block should measure 6½" x 6½".

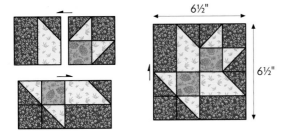

8 Repeat steps 1–7 to make a total of 85 blocks.

Constructing the Quilt

After completing the center of the quilt, always measure the length and width before cutting borders. Refer to "Measuring for Borders" on page 93.

1 Lay out the blocks, light sashing rectangles, and brown 2" cornerstones in an on-point setting, with seven blocks across and seven blocks down. Rearrange until you are pleased with the color placement.

2 Sew the cornerstones and sashing rectangles together to create the sashing rows as indicated in the quilt assembly diagram. Press the seam allowances toward the sashing strips and place the strips back in your layout.

3 Sew pieced blocks and sashing rectangles together to create rows. Press the seam allowances toward the sashing strips. Place the block rows back in your quilt layout.

4 Sew a sashing row and a block row together before adding the side setting triangles to each end of the row. Press seam allowances toward the sashing rows and setting triangles. Sew a sashing row to each side of the center block row, but do not add the corner triangles yet.

5 Sew the rows together. Press the seam allowances toward the center row.

6 Add the corner triangles and press the seam allowances toward the triangles.

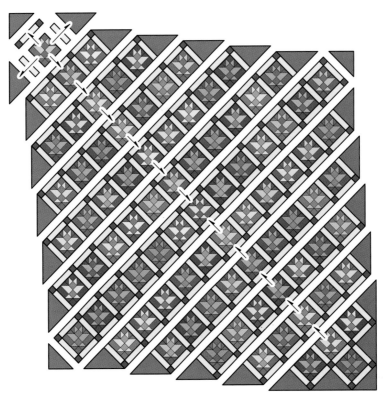

Quilt assembly

7 To make the inner border, trim the selvages from the brown 2" x 42" strips and sew the strips together end to end. Press the seam allowances to one side. From this strip cut two strips, 77" long, for the side borders and two strips, 80" long, for the top and bottom borders. Attach the side borders first, press the seam allowances toward the border strips, and then add the top and bottom borders. Press.

8 Attach the dark-red 8½" x 80" strips to the sides of the quilt top and press the seam allowances toward the red border. Add the dark-red 8½" x 96" strips to the top and bottom. Press.

Finishing the Quilt

1 Layer the quilt top with the batting and backing. Quilt by hand or machine. The featured quilt was machine quilted with feather motifs designed to fit in the blocks, sashing, setting triangles, and outer border.

2 Add binding using the 1⅞"-wide strips. If you need additional details, go to ShopMartingale.com for free downloadable information.

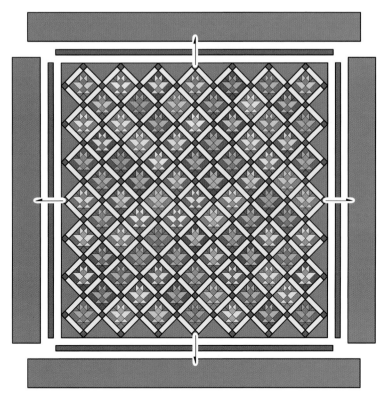

Adding borders

Civil War Generals

Its proximity to the Mississippi River as well as valuable lead-ore mines made Galena, Illinois, one of the most important cities in the state prior to the Civil War. It has received most of its attention, though, because it was the home of nine Civil War generals.

That list of generals included Augustus Louis Chetlain, the first man from Illinois to volunteer for the Union army, and Ely Samuel Parker, aide-de-camp to Ulysses S. Grant and transcriber of the Appomattox surrender terms. The most notable general, however, was Ulysses S. Grant himself. A graduate of West Point, Grant was living in Galena and working in his father's leather shop when the war began.

After leading the Union armies to victory, Grant returned home a war hero and remained in Galena until 1869, when he became the 18th president of the United States. Joining him in Washington, D.C., were fellow Galena residents General John Aaron Rawlins, who served as Grant's secretary of war, and prominent abolitionist Elihu Washburne, who became Grant's secretary of state.

The nine generals are represented by the nine stars in the official flag of Galena, Illinois.

Flag of the city of Galena, Illinois

FINISHED QUILT: 84½" x 84½" ✳ FINISHED BLOCK: 6" x 6"

"Civil War Generals," designed by Paula Barnes, pieced by Robin Sutherlin,
and machine quilted by Sharon Dixon

Materials

Yardage is based on 42"-wide fabric.

2⅞ yards of red print for pieced cornerstones,
  setting triangles, and outer border

2 yards of light print for blocks, pieced cornerstones,
  and inner border

1⅞ yards of tan print for sashing

⅓ yard of cheddar print for blocks

⅛ yard or 9" x 11" piece *each* of 21 assorted dark
  prints for blocks

1 yard of fabric for binding

7¾ yards of fabric for backing

90" x 90" piece of batting

Cutting

From *each* of the 21 assorted dark prints, cut:
  4 rectangles, 2½" x 8"

From the light print, cut:
  17 strips, 2½" x 42"; crosscut 9 of the strips into
    42 rectangles, 2½" x 8"
  13 strips, 1½" x 42"

From the cheddar print, cut:
  4 strips, 2½" x 42"

From the red print, cut:
  5 strips, 1½" x 42"
  2 strips, 7½" x 84½", on the *lengthwise* grain*
  2 strips, 7½" x 70½", on the *lengthwise* grain*

** Cut the lengthwise border strips 2" to 3" longer than
specified; do not cut to the final length until the quilt center is
complete and you have determined the final measurements.*

From the *remainder* of the red print, cut:

- 5 squares, 9¾" x 9¾"; cut into quarters diagonally to make 20 triangles
- 6 squares, 4⅛" x 4⅛"; cut into quarters diagonally to make 24 triangles
- 2 squares, 5⅛" x 5⅛"; cut in half diagonally to make 4 triangles

From the tan print, cut:

- 24 strips, 2½" x 42"; crosscut into 144 rectangles, 2½" x 6½"

From the binding fabric, cut:

- 9 strips, 1⅞" x 42"

Making the Nine Patch Blocks

1 Sew two matching dark 2½" x 8" rectangles and one light 2½" x 8" rectangle together and press seam allowances toward the dark rectangles. Make two. Cut three 2½"-wide segments from each strip set for a total of six identical segments. Repeat with the remaining dark and light 2½" x 8" rectangles for a total of 126 segments. Keep the matching segments together.

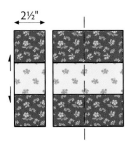

2½"

Make 2 strip sets.
Cut 6 segments.

2 Sew two light 2½" x 42" strips and one cheddar 2½" x 42" strip together and press the seam allowances toward the cheddar print. Make four strip sets. Cut the strip sets into 2½"-wide segments for a total of 61 segments.

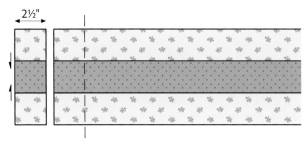

2½"

Make 4 strip sets.
Cut 61 segments.

3 Sew two matching segments from step 1 and one segment from step 2 together to make a Nine Patch block. Press seam allowances as indicated by the arrows. Make a total of 61 blocks. (You'll have four segments from step 1 left over.)

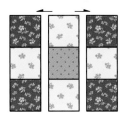 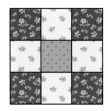

Make 61 .

Making the Pieced Cornerstones

1 Sew one light 1½" x 42" strip and one red 1½" x 42" strip together and press seam allowances toward the red print. Make five strip sets. Cut into 1½"-wide segments for a total of 120 segments.

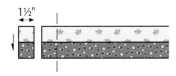

Make 5 strip sets.
Cut 120 segments.

2 Sew two segments together to make a four-patch unit. Press seam allowances as indicated by the arrows. Repeat to make a total of 60 four-patch cornerstones.

Make 60.

Constructing the Quilt

After completing the center of the quilt, always measure the length and width before cutting borders. Refer to "Measuring for Borders" on page 93.

1 Lay out the blocks, tan sashing rectangles, and pieced cornerstones in an on-point setting, with six blocks across and six blocks down. Rearrange the blocks until you are pleased with the color placement. Note the alternating orientation of the cornerstones throughout the layout.

2 Sew the cornerstones, sashing rectangles, and small red triangles together to create the sashing rows. Press the seam allowances toward the sashing rectangles. Place the sashing rows back in the layout.

3 Sew the Nine Patch blocks and sashing rectangles together to create rows. Add a side setting triangle to each end of the row as needed. Press the seam allowances toward the sashing strips and triangles. Place the block rows back in the layout.

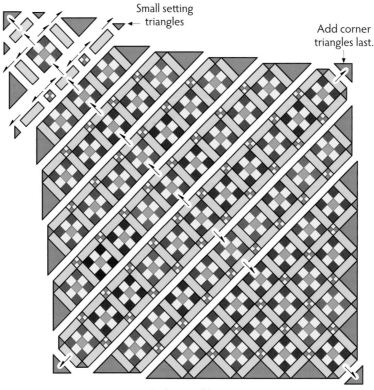

Small setting triangles

Add corner triangles last.

Quilt assembly

4 Sew a sashing row and a block row together. Press seam allowances toward the sashing. Sew the rows together. Press the seam allowances as indicated by the arrows, away from the center row.

5 Add the corner triangles and press the seam allowances toward the triangles.

6 For the inner border, trim the selvages from the remaining light 1½" x 42" strips and sew the strips together end to end. Press the seam allowances to one side. From this strip cut two strips, 68½" long, for the side borders and two strips, 70½" long, for the top and bottom borders. Attach the side borders first and press the seam allowances toward the border strips. Then add the top and bottom borders and press in the same manner.

7 Attach the red 7½" x 70½" strips to the sides of the quilt top and press the seam allowances toward the red border. Add the red 7½" x 84½" strips to the top and bottom. Press.

Finishing the Quilt

1 Layer the quilt top with the batting and backing. Quilt by hand or machine. The featured quilt was machine quilted with an allover feather design.

2 Add binding using the 1⅞"-wide strips. If you need additional details, go to ShopMartingale.com for free downloadable information.

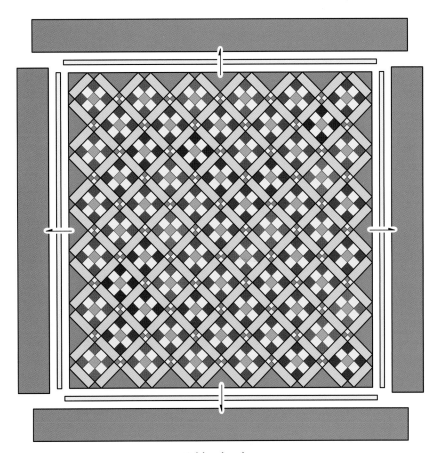

Adding borders

Cabin Creek

The Cabin Creek battlefield in the Cherokee Nation (present-day Big Cabin, Oklahoma) was the site of not one, but two Civil War battles. The Confederate army initiated both events in an attempt to disrupt the Union army supply trains, but in neither case did the Confederate forces achieve the desired results.

The first battle of Cabin Creek, on July 1 and 2, 1863, was significant historically because it was the first time that black soldiers (The First Kansas Colored Infantry) fought alongside white troops in turning back Confederate troops. Hollywood's 1989 film *Glory,* incorrectly billed as the "story of America's first unit of black soldiers during the Civil War," depicts the 54th Massachusetts Volunteer Infantry in battle at Fort Wagner, South Carolina, for this historic event, but that event actually occurred later in July of the same year, after the Cabin Creek battle.

Against the wishes of the Union secretary of war, Kansas senator and recruiter James H. Lane began recruiting black soldiers in June of 1862. The First Kansas Colored Infantry was mustered in as a battalion on July 13, 1863, at Fort Scott, Kansas. They were the first to see action and the first to die in battle.

In 1866, after the Civil War, Congress authorized six black regiments to serve in Oklahoma and the Indian Territory. Many of the soldiers from the First Kansas also served in these regiments. In later years, these regiments would be called "Buffalo Soldiers," a name given to them by the Plains Indians because the curly black hair of the soldiers reminded them of the mane of the buffalo.

Buffalo soldiers

FINISHED QUILT: 81½" x 99½" ✳ FINISHED BLOCK: 9" x 9"
"Cabin Creek," designed by Paula Barnes, pieced by Mary Ellen Robison,
and machine quilted by Sharon Dixon

Materials

Yardage is based on 42"-wide fabric.

3⅛ yards of dark-brown print for first and fifth
  borders

1 yard of cream print for second and fourth borders

⅓ yard *each* of 15 assorted pink prints and brown
  prints for blocks and pieced third border

⅓ yard *each* of 15 assorted light prints for blocks
  and pieced third border

1 yard of brown print for binding

7¾ yards of fabric for backing

87" x 105" piece of batting

3" finished "Star Singles" papers* (optional)

*See "Using Star Singles" on page 31 before cutting fabrics.

Cutting

*Do not cut the lengthwise border strips from the
dark-brown print until the quilt center is complete
and you have determined the final measurements.*

From *each* of the 15 assorted light prints, cut:
  8 squares, 4¼" x 4¼"*

From *each of 12* assorted light prints, cut:
  2 squares, 6⅞" x 6⅞"; cut in half diagonally to
    make 4 triangles
  4 squares, 3⅞" x 3⅞"; cut in half diagonally to
    make 8 triangles

**From *each* of the 15 assorted pink and brown
  prints, cut:**
  8 squares, 4¼" x 4¼"*

* See "Using Star Singles" on page 31 before cutting.

From *each of 12* assorted pink or brown prints, cut:
  2 squares, 6⅞" x 6⅞"; cut in half diagonally to make 4 triangles
  4 squares, 3⅞" x 3⅞"; cut in half diagonally to make 8 triangles

From *each of 4* assorted pink or brown prints, cut:
  1 square, 3½" x 3½"

From the dark-brown print, cut:
  7 strips, 2" x 42"

From the remainder of the dark-brown print, cut on the *lengthwise* grain:
  2 strips, 6½" x 81½"
  2 strips, 6½" x 87½"

From the cream print, cut:
  15 strips, 2" x 42"

From the brown print for binding, cut:
  10 strips, 1⅞" x 42", or 1⅞"-wide bias strips to total 400"

Using Star Singles

If you use the 3" Star Singles papers, do not cut the 4¼" squares. Instead, cut the following pieces.

From *each* of the 15 light and 15 pink and brown prints, cut:
2 squares, 8½" x 8½"

Making the Half-Square-Triangle Units

Referring to "Half-Square-Triangle Units" on page 91, mark the light 4¼" squares and layer them right sides together with the pink or brown 4¼" squares. Sew, cut, press seam allowances toward the darker print, and trim to 3½" x 3½". Make 240 half-square-triangle units (four will be extra).

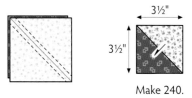

Make 240.

Making the Blocks

1 Add light and/or pink or brown 3⅞" triangles to the half-square-triangle units as shown. Make 48 of each unit.

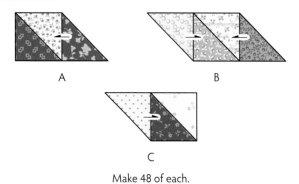

A   B

C

Make 48 of each.

2 Sew one each of the units from step 1 together for one block.

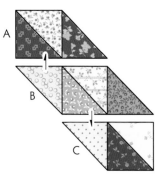

A

B

C

3 Fold a light and a pink or brown 6⅞" triangle in half and gently press on each fold to mark the center. Be careful not to stretch the bias edges.

4 Align the fold of each triangle with the center of the pieced section from step 2. Pin in place and sew. Be sure the light triangle is sewn next to the smaller pink or brown triangles, and the pink or brown triangle is sewn next to the smaller light triangles.

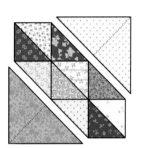 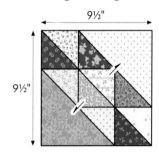

5 Repeat steps 2–4 to make 48 blocks.

Making the Pieced Border

1 Sew 20 half-square-triangle units and two pink or brown 3½" squares together to create the top pieced border. Press all seam allowances away from the center. Repeat to make a border for the bottom.

Make 2.

2 Sew 26 half-square-triangle units together to create a side border. Press seam allowances away from the center. Make two.

Make 2.

Constructing the Quilt

After completing the center of the quilt, always measure the length and width before cutting borders. Refer to "Measuring for Borders" on page 93.

1 Lay out the blocks in eight rows of six blocks in each. Rearrange until you are pleased with the color placement. Note that the blocks are rotated from block to block and from row to row to form the quilt pattern.

2 Sew the blocks together into rows as indicated in the quilt assembly diagram. Press the seam allowances toward the large pink or brown triangle in the adjacent block. Place the block rows back in your quilt layout.

3 Sew the rows together in groups of two and then sew these pairs of rows together. Press the seam allowances as indicated by the arrows.

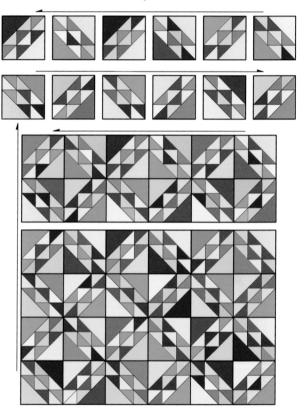

Quilt assembly

4 For the first border, trim the selvages from the brown 2" x 42" strips and sew the strips together end to end. Press the seam allowances to one side. From this strip cut two strips, 72½" long, for the side borders and two strips, 57½" long, for the top and bottom borders. Attach the side borders first, press the seam allowances toward the border strips, and then add the top and bottom borders. Press.

5 For the second border, trim the selvages from the cream 2" x 42" strips and sew the strips together end to end. Press the seam allowances to one side. From this strip cut two strips, 75½" long, for the side borders and two strips, 60½" long, for the top and bottom borders. Attach the side borders first, press the seam allowances toward the first border, and then add the top and bottom borders. Press. Set the remainder of the pieced strip aside for the fourth border.

6 Attach the pieced borders without squares to the sides of the quilt top, making sure the cream triangles are joined to the cream border. Press the seam allowances toward the cream border. Add the pieced borders with squares to the top and bottom in the same manner and press.

7 Using the remaining pieced cream strip from step 5, cut two strips, 84½" long, for the sides of the fourth border and two strips, 69½" long, for the top and bottom. Attach the side borders first, press the seam allowances toward the cream strips, and then add the top and bottom borders. Press.

8 Attach the brown 6½" x 87½" strips to the sides of the quilt top and press the seam allowances toward the brown fifth border. Add the brown 6½" x 81½" strips to the top and bottom. Press.

Finishing the Quilt

1 Layer the quilt top with the batting and backing. Quilt by hand or machine. The featured quilt was machine quilted with an allover concentric feather design.

2 Add binding using the 1⅞"-wide strips. If you need additional details, go to ShopMartingale.com for free downloadable information.

Adding borders

Plantation Road

A Scotland-to-Savannah success story, Henry McAlpin was born in 1777 and immigrated to the United States in his mid-30s, settling in Georgia. In 1815, he received the 400-acre Hermitage Plantation as a gift from friend William I. Scott, who had purchased the estate at auction. McAlpin and his family moved into their new home on the banks of the Savannah River, and McAlpin began strategically building a multifaceted business, not just an agricultural enterprise. The plantation produced rice, lumber, and cast-iron products, and in 1819, McAlpin added a brick-manufacturing plant. Hermitage's bricks, called "Savannah gray bricks," were used to rebuild Savannah after a massive fire in 1820.

More than 200 slaves resided at Hermitage Plantation, and McAlpin used them to maintain a positive cash flow for his many businesses. Slaves were bought, sold, traded, and often used as collateral, but McAlpin was not considered a harsh master by nineteenth-century standards. He allowed older slaves who could no longer work to remain on the plantation, and he kept slave families intact.

McAlpin spurned the "gang system" of labor, in which slaves worked from sunup to sundown, in favor of the "task system." With this approach, work was divided into individual tasks, and when the task was completed, the work for the day was done. This allowed slaves time to work on other activities to assist their own families.

Slave quarters

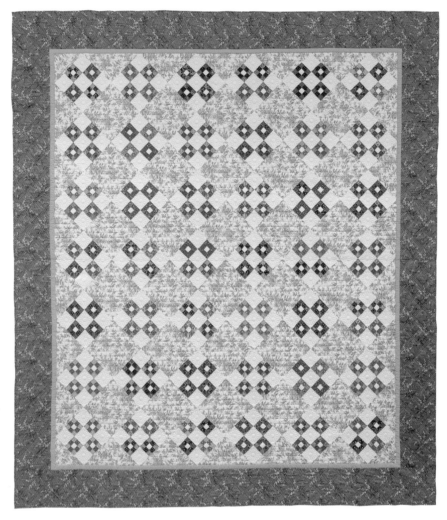

FINISHED QUILT: 95" x 107½" ✳ FINISHED BLOCK: 9" x 9"
"Plantation Road," designed by Paula Barnes, pieced by Mary Ellen Robison, and
machine quilted by Marcella Pickett and Margie Love of Crooked Creek Quilts

Materials

Yardage is based on 42"-wide fabric.

3½ yards of red toile for alternate blocks and setting
    triangles

2¾ yards of dark large-scale floral for outer border

2½ yards of cream tone on tone or solid for
    pieced blocks

½ yard of pink print for inner border

¼ yard or 1 fat quarter *each* of 14 assorted brown
    prints for pieced blocks

¼ yard or 1 fat quarter *each* of 14 assorted medium
    prints in teal, red, pink, and tan for pieced blocks

1 yard of fabric for binding

9 yards of fabric for backing

103" x 116" piece of batting

Cutting

*Do not cut the lengthwise border strips from the
large-scale floral until the quilt center is complete and
you have determined the final measurements.*

From the cream tone on tone, cut:
    19 strips, 3½" x 42"; crosscut into 210 squares,
        3½" x 3½"
    9 strips, 1½" x 42"; crosscut into 42 rectangles,
        1½" x 7"

From *each* of the 14 assorted brown prints, cut:
    12 rectangles, 1½" x 7"

From *each* of the 14 assorted medium prints, cut:
    12 rectangles, 1½" x 7"

From the red toile, cut:

6 squares, 14" x 14"; cut into quarters diagonally to make 24 triangles (2 will be extra)

30 squares, 9½" x 9½"

2 squares, 7¼" x 7¼"; cut in half diagonally to make 4 triangles

From the pink print, cut:

9 strips, 1½" x 42"

From the dark large-scale floral, cut on the _lengthwise_ grain:

2 strips, 8½" x 91½"

2 strips, 8½" x 95"

From the binding fabric, cut:

11 strips, 1⅞" x 42", or bias strips to total 440"

Making the Blocks

1 Sew two matching medium 1½" x 7" rectangles and one brown 1½" x 7" rectangle together and press seam allowances toward the brown print. Make two matching strip sets. Cut four segments, 1½" wide, from each strip set for a total of eight segments.

1½"

Make 2 strip sets.
Cut 8 segments.

2 Sew two 1½" x 7" rectangles of the same brown print used in step 1, to a cream 1½" x 7" rectangle. Press seam allowances toward the brown print. Cut four segments, 1½" wide.

1½"

Make 1 strip set.
Cut 4 segments.

3 Sew the segments from steps 1 and 2 together to make four identical nine-patch units. Press as indicated.

Make 4.

4 Sew the four nine-patch units together with five cream 3½" squares to make the Double Nine Patch block. Press as indicated.

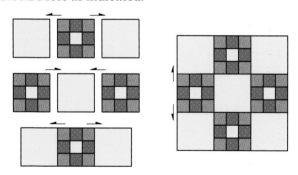

5 Repeat steps 1–4 to make a total of 42 blocks. Note that some blocks include two different nine-patch units. Make several nine-patch units, and then combine them with others when assembling the Double Nine Patch blocks.

Constructing the Quilt

After completing the center of the quilt, always measure the length and width before cutting borders. Refer to "Measuring for Borders" on page 93.

1 Lay out the blocks in an on-point setting with six blocks across and seven blocks down, adding the red-toile alternate blocks and setting triangles. Rearrange the Double Nine Patch blocks until you are pleased with the color placement.

2 Sew the blocks together into diagonal rows as indicated in the quilt assembly diagram. Press the seam allowances toward the alternate blocks and triangles. Place the rows back in the layout.

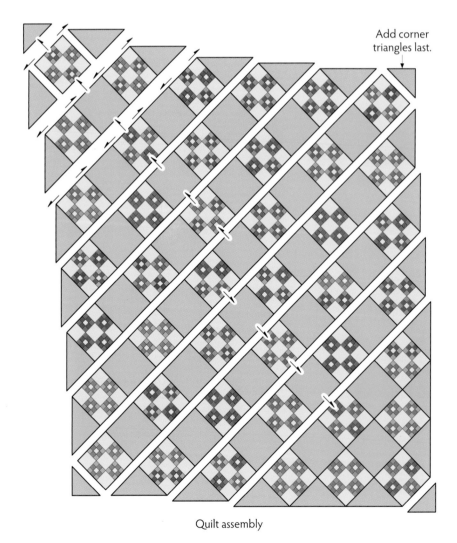

Add corner triangles last.

Quilt assembly

3 Sew the rows together. Press the seam allowances as indicated by the arrows.

4 Add the corner triangles and press the seam allowances toward the triangles.

5 For the inner border, trim the selvages from the pink 1½" x 42" strips and sew the strips together end to end. Press seam allowances to one side. From this strip cut two strips, 89½" long, for the side borders and two strips, 79" long, for the top and bottom borders. Attach the side borders first, press the seam allowances toward the border strips, and then add the top and bottom borders. Press.

6 Attach the floral 8½" x 91½" strips to the sides of the quilt top and press the seam allowances toward the floral border. Add the floral 8½" x 95" strips to the top and bottom. Press.

Finishing the Quilt

1 Layer the quilt top with the batting and backing. Quilt by hand or machine. The featured quilt was machine quilted with a flower motif in the squares of the Double Nine Patch blocks, single crosshatching in the background and setting triangles, and double crosshatching in the outer border.

2 Add binding using the 1⅞"-wide strips. If you need additional details, go to ShopMartingale.com for free downloadable information.

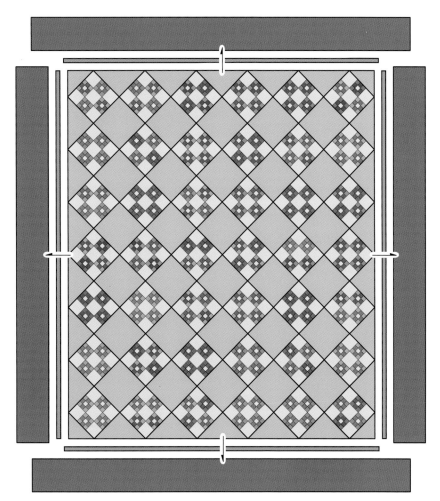

Adding borders

Kennesaw Mountain

Not all action in the Civil War took place on the battlefield; one intriguing episode occurred on the railroad tracks. On April 12, 1862, James Andrews, a civilian scout for the Union army, along with another civilian, Bill Campbell, and 22 volunteers from three Ohio regiments, stole a passenger train as it headed from Atlanta northward to Chattanooga. Their plan was to damage or destroy tracks and telegraph wires, thus disrupting the supply lines serving the Confederate army.

While the train was stopped for a fuel-and-meal break at Big Shanty (now Kennesaw, Georgia), Andrews and his men boarded the train and stole its locomotive, named The General, plus a passenger car. Big Shanty didn't have a telegraph office so other towns along the route couldn't be alerted.

The train from the Great Locomotive Chase

When Conductor William Allen Fuller saw his train pull away from the station—with some alarm, one might imagine!—he and two other men began pursuit. For several miles they chased The General, partly on foot and partly by use of a handcar. Eventually Fuller was able to commandeer a southbound train called The Texas, running it backward after The General for 51 miles. After a journey of 87 miles, The General lost power. Andrews and his men scattered into the woods, but were ultimately captured.

Andrews' Raid, or "the Great Locomotive Chase" as it came to be called, had failed to cause as much railway damage as intended, and the Confederates executed Andrews as a spy on June 7, 1862. Some of the raiders were later awarded the Medal of Honor by the US Congress, but Andrews was a civilian and therefore ineligible for such recognition.

After a long legal battle and many claims of ownership, The General is now a fixture at the Big Shanty Museum (Southern Museum of Civil War and Locomotive History) in Kennesaw, Georgia.

FINISHED QUILT: 92½" x 92½" ✳ FINISHED BLOCK: 12" x 12"
"Kennesaw Mountain," designed by Paula Barnes, pieced by Mary Ellen Robison,
and machine quilted by Marcella Pickett and Margie Love of Crooked Creek Quilts

Materials

Yardage is based on 42"-wide fabric.

3 yards of border print or floral for fourth border

3 yards of light print for block backgrounds and
   pieced second border

2 yards of red print for first and third borders and
   pieced second border

½ yard *each* of 15 assorted dark prints for blocks

⅜ yard *each* of 8 assorted light prints for blocks

⅞ yard of fabric for binding

9 yards of fabric for backing

100" x 100" piece of batting

2" finished "Star Singles" papers* (optional)

See "Using Star Singles" on page 43 before cutting fabrics.

Cutting

From *each* of the 15 assorted dark prints, cut:
   26 rectangles, 2" x 3½" (6 will be extra)

**From the remainder of the 15 dark prints, cut *a
total of*:**
   25 pairs of matching squares, 5¾" x 5¾"
   25 squares, 3½" x 3½"
   3 squares, 5½" x 5½"; cut into quarters diagonally
      to make 12 triangles
   2 squares, 3" x 3"; cut in half diagonally to make
      4 triangles

From *each* of the 8 assorted light prints, cut:
   96 squares, 2" x 2"

From the light print for background and border, cut:

8 strips, 5¾" x 42"; crosscut into 50 squares, 5¾" x 5¾"

2 strips, 7⅝" x 42"; crosscut into 8 squares, 7⅝" x 7⅝". Cut into quarters diagonally to make 32 triangles.

2 strips, 5" x 42"; crosscut into 12 squares, 5" x 5"

6 strips, 3¼" x 42"; crosscut into 72 squares, 3¼" x 3¼"*

From the red print, cut:

6 strips, 3¼" x 42"; crosscut into 72 squares, 3¼" x 3¼"*

4 squares, 2½" x 2½"

16 strips, 2½" x 42"

From the border print or floral, cut on the *lengthwise* grain:

4 strips, 6½" x 98"

From the binding fabric, cut:

10 strips, 1⅞" x 42"

*See "Using Star Singles" below before cutting fabrics.

Using Star Singles

If you use the 2" Star Singles papers, do not cut the 3¼" squares. Instead, cut the following pieces.

From *both* the light print and the red print, cut:

3 strips, 6½" x 42"; crosscut 18 squares, 6½" x 6½"

Making the Blocks

1 Using a pencil, draw a straight line from corner to corner on the wrong side of the assorted light 2" squares.

2 With right sides together, place a marked light square on one end of a dark 2" x 3½" rectangle. Sew on the line and trim, leaving a ¼" seam allowance. Press the seam allowances toward the light print. Repeat to add a matching light square on the other end of the rectangle. Sew, trim, and press to

complete a flying-geese unit. Repeat to make a total of 384 flying-geese units.

Make 384.

3 Place all of the units into a paper grocery bag. Close the bag and SHAKE!

4 Pull three flying-geese units out of the bag and sew them together as shown. Press seam allowances in one direction. Make a total of 128 rows.

Make 128.

5 Referring to "Half-Square-Triangle Units" on page 91, mark the light 5¾" squares and layer them right sides together with the assorted dark 5¾" squares. Sew, cut, press seam allowances toward the darker print, and trim to 5" x 5". Make 100 half-square-triangle units.

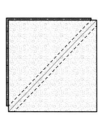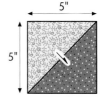

Make 100.

6 Arrange four matching half-square-triangle units, four flying-geese rows, and one assorted dark 3½" square in three rows as shown. Sew the units into rows and press seam allowances as indicated by the arrows. Sew the rows together and press. Make 25 blocks.

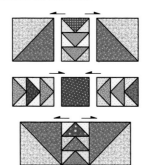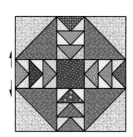

Make 25.

Making the Pieced Setting Triangles

1 Arrange two flying-geese rows, two light 7⅝" triangles, one dark 5½" triangle, and one light 5" square as shown. Sew them together in rows and then sew the rows together. Press seam allowances as indicated by the arrows. Make 12 pieced side setting triangles.

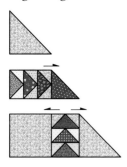 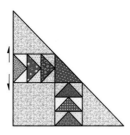

Make 12.

2 Arrange one flying-geese row, two light 7⅝" triangles, and one dark 3" triangle together as shown. Sew the light triangles to the flying-geese row and then add the dark triangle. Press seam allowances as indicated by the arrows. Make four pieced corner setting triangles.

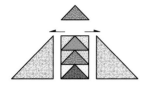 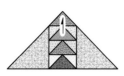

Make 4.

Making the Pieced Border

1 Referring to "Half-Square-Triangle Units," mark the light 3¼" squares and layer them right sides together with the red 3¼" squares. Sew, cut, press seam allowances toward the red print, and trim to 2½" x 2½". Make 144 half-square-triangle units.

2½"

2½"

Make 144.

2 Sew 36 half-square-triangle units together as shown to create a side border. Make two. Press seam allowances away from the center. Sew 36 half-square-triangle units and two red 2½" squares together as shown to create the top pieced border. Press all seam allowances away from the center. Repeat to make a second border for the bottom. Set aside until you are ready to add the pieced border to the quilt.

Make 2 of each.

Constructing the Quilt

After completing the center of the quilt, always measure the length and width before cutting borders. Refer to "Measuring for Borders" on page 93.

1 Lay out the blocks in an on-point setting, with four blocks across and four blocks down. Add the side and corner setting triangles to the layout. Rearrange the blocks and triangles until you are pleased with the color placement.

2 Sew the blocks together into rows as indicated in the quilt assembly diagram. Press the seam allowances in opposite directions from row to row. Place the block rows back in your quilt layout.

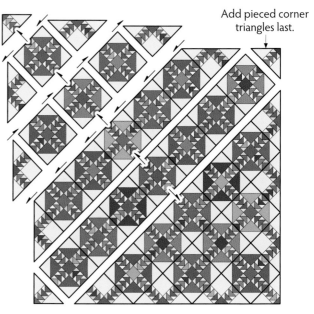

Add pieced corner triangles last.

Quilt assembly

3 Sew the rows together. Press the seam allowances away from the center row, as indicated by the arrows. Add the corner triangles last.

4 For the first border, trim the selvages from the red 2½" x 42" strips and sew the strips together end to end. Press the seam allowances to one side. From this strip cut two strips, 68½" long, for the side borders and two strips, 72½" long, for the top and bottom borders. Attach the side borders first, press the seam allowances toward the border strips, and then add the top and bottom borders. Press. Set the remainder of the pieced strip aside for the third border.

5 Sew the pieced borders without squares to the sides of the quilt top, with the light triangles toward the quilt center. Press seam allowances toward the red border. Sew the pieced borders with squares to the top and bottom in the same manner and press.

6 Using the remaining pieced red strip from step 4, cut two strips, 76½" long, for the sides of the third border and two strips, 80½" long, for the top and bottom. Attach the side borders first, press the seam allowances toward the red strips, and then add the top and bottom borders. Press.

7 Referring to "Mitered Borders" on page 91, add the border-print strips to all four sides of the quilt and miter the corners. Press.

Finishing the Quilt

1 Layer the quilt top with the batting and backing. Quilt by hand or machine. The featured quilt was machine quilted to highlight the elements of the design, including curved diamonds at the center of each block and feathers placed to fit in the block triangles and the background.

2 Add binding using the 1⅞"-wide strips. If you need additional details, go to ShopMartingale.com for free downloadable information.

Adding borders

Lancaster

William Penn's Pennsylvania began as a colony founded on freedom of conscience and religious liberty. As such, it quickly became a home for Quakers and other persecuted religious minorities. Quakers were among the earliest settlers in Lancaster, and they played a major role in the abolition movement in both the United States and Great Britain.

A large part of those antislavery activities consisted of helping slaves escape through what Levi Coffin, himself a Quaker, called a "mysterious road," or Underground Railroad. The passage of the Fugitive Slave Act of 1793, and the risk of prosecution if caught assisting an escaping slave, did not deter most Quakers. Instead, it forced them to become more secretive, and the Underground Railroad flourished from 1850 to1860.

As a young child in North Carolina, Levi Coffin was exposed to slavery and was strongly opposed to it. In 1826, he moved to Indiana to escape the slaveholders' persecution of Quakers. As a wealthy businessman, he was able to provide considerable funds to support the Underground Railroad operations in his area. Coffin became known to Confederate slave owners as the "President of the Underground Railroad." In 1847, he moved to Cincinnati to manage a warehouse that sold only goods produced by free labor.

Levi Coffin, "President" of the Underground Railroad

With the abolition of slavery at the end of the Civil War, Coffin traveled around the United States, France, and Great Britain, raising funds to start aid societies to assist freed slaves. In 1876, his book *Reminiscences of Levi Coffin* was published. In it he said, "I resign my office and declare the operations of the Underground Railroad at an end." Historians consider his book to be one of the best firsthand accounts of the activities of the Underground Railroad. Coffin is estimated to have helped between 2,000 and 3,000 slaves escape. Coffin died on September 17, 1877.

FINISHED QUILT: 85½" x 93½" ✳ **FINISHED BLOCK:** 6" x 6"

"Lancaster," designed by Paula Barnes, pieced by Mary Ellen Robison, and
machine quilted by Marcella Pickett and Margie Love of Crooked Creek Quilts

Materials

Yardage is based on 42"-wide fabric.

4 yards of black print for inner and outer borders
and pieced middle border

2¼ yards of cheddar print for setting triangles

1½ yards of light print for pieced middle border

⅛ yard or 1 fat eighth *each* of 30 assorted light prints
for blocks

⅛ yard or 1 fat eighth *each* of 30 assorted medium to
dark prints in red, brown, black, and cheddar for
blocks

1 yard of black print for binding*

**If you want to use the same black print for borders and
binding, you'll need 5 yards total.*

8 yards of fabric for backing

92" x 100" piece of batting

2" finished "Star Singles" papers** (optional)

**See "Using Star Singles" on page 49 before cutting fabrics.

Cutting

*Do not cut the lengthwise border strips from the black
print until the quilt center is complete and you have
determined the final measurements.*

**From *each* of the 30 assorted medium to dark
prints, cut:**

2 squares, 2½" x 2½"

2 rectangles, 1½" x 6½"

8 rectangles, 1½" x 2½"

16 squares, 1½" x 1½"

From *each* of the 30 assorted light prints, cut:
　　2 rectangles, 1½" x 6½"
　　16 rectangles, 1½" x 2½"
From the cheddar print, cut:
　　7 strips, 9¾" x 42"; crosscut into 27 squares,
　　　　9¾" x 9¾". Cut into quarters diagonally to
　　　　make 108 triangles (2 are extra).
　　1 strip, 5⅛" x 42"; crosscut into 6 squares,
　　　　5⅛" x 5⅛". Cut in half diagonally to make 12
　　　　triangles.
From the black print for borders, cut:
　　12 strips, 3¼" x 42"; crosscut into 140 squares,
　　　　3¼" x 3¼"*
　　4 squares, 2½" x 2½"
From the *remainder* of the black print, cut on the
　　***lengthwise* grain:**
　　2 strips, 7" x 80½"
　　2 strips, 7" x 85½"
　　2 strips, 2½" x 64½"
　　2 strips, 2¾" x 68½"
From the light print for pieced border, cut:
　　12 strips, 3¼" x 42"; crosscut into 140 squares,
　　　　3¼" x 3¼"*
　　4 squares, 2½" x 2½"
From the black binding fabric, cut:
　　10 strips, 1⅞" x 42", or bias strips to total 400"

*See "Using Star Singles" below before cutting fabrics.

Using Star Singles

If you use the 2" Star Singles papers for the pieced border, do not cut the 3¼" squares. Instead, cut the following pieces.

From *both* the black print and the light print, cut:
　　6 strips, 6½" x 42"; crosscut 35 squares,
　　　　6½" x 6½"

Making the Blocks

For each block, choose one light print and three medium to dark prints in the following sizes.

- **Light for background:** 1 rectangle, 1½" x 6½", and 8 rectangles, 1½" x 2½"
- **Medium/dark for squares:** 1 rectangle, 1½" x 6½", and 1 square, 2½" x 2½"
- **Medium/dark for rectangles:** 4 rectangles, 1½" x 2½"
- **Medium/dark for star points:** 8 squares, 1½" x 1½"

1 Sew a medium or dark 1½" x 6½" rectangle and a light 1½" x 6½" rectangle together. Press seam allowances toward the light rectangle. Cut into four segments, 1½" wide.

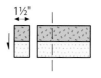

Cut 4 segments.

2 Sew a segment from step 1 to a matching light 1½" x 2½" rectangle and press the seam allowances toward the just-added rectangle. Make four identical units.

Make 4.

3 Using a pencil or fabric marker, draw a line from corner to corner on the wrong side of the eight matching medium or dark 1½" squares.

4 With right sides together, place a marked square on one end of a light 1½" x 2½" rectangle. Sew on the line and trim, leaving a ¼" seam allowance. Press the seam allowances toward the dark print. Repeat to add a second square on the other end of the rectangle. Make four identical flying-geese units.

Make 4.

5 Sew a flying-geese unit and a medium or dark 1½" x 2½" rectangle together. Press seam allowances toward the rectangle. Make four of these units.

Make 4.

6 Arrange the pieced units from step 5, the units from step 2, and the medium or dark 2½" square as shown. Sew the units together in rows and press as indicated by the arrows. Sew the rows together and press. The block should measure 6½" x 6½".

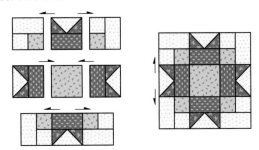

7 Repeat steps 1–6 to make 60 blocks.

Constructing the Quilt

Work on a design wall or other flat surface to arrange your blocks. You'll cut eight of the blocks in half after determining your layout.

1 Arrange the blocks on point in seven vertical rows. Four rows will have nine blocks and three rows will have eight blocks. Place the cheddar setting triangles in the layout to help with color placement, and refer to the assembly diagram on page 52 for guidance.

2 When you are pleased with the arrangement, remove one of the blocks that needs to be cut in half. Using a pencil and a ruler that is at least 9½" long, draw a diagonal line on the right side of the block, ¼" from the center diagonal. (Do not mark the centerline.) Sew a line of straight stitches ⅛" from the pencil line within the ¼" seam allowance. This will keep the block seams from opening up and will help to stabilize the bias edges.

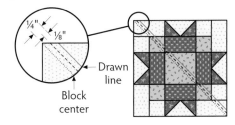

3 Using a ruler and rotary cutter, cut on the pencil line. Place the half block with stitching back in the layout and repeat to cut the remaining seven blocks. Discard the smaller pieced triangles or save them for a future creative project.

4 Sew a half block to a 9¾" triangle to make the end row unit as shown. Press the seam allowances toward the cheddar triangle. Repeat for each of the eight half blocks and return the units to the layout.

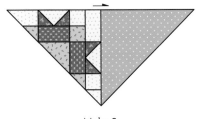

Make 8.

5 For the three rows without half blocks, sew one 9¾" triangle and two 5⅛" triangles to an end block as shown. Make six end units.

6 Sew each of the remaining blocks together with two 9¾" setting triangles to make row units. Press all seam allowances toward the cheddar triangles.

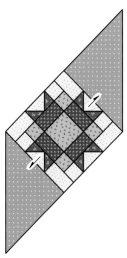

7 Sew the row units and end units together to make the rows. Press the seam allowances in one direction.

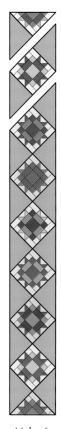

Make 4.   Make 3.

Perfect Piecing

To accurately join blocks and triangles as called for in steps 5 and 6, place the block right sides together with the triangle, aligning the right-angle corners. Sew with a scant ¼" seam allowance.

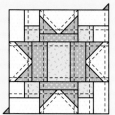

8 Sew the rows together to complete the quilt center. Press seam allowances toward the rows without half blocks.

Making the Pieced Border

The pieced borders feature a combination of two different four-patch block units.

1 Referring to "Half-Square-Triangle Units" on page 91, mark the light 3¼" squares and layer them right sides together with the black 3¼" squares. Sew, cut, press seam allowances toward the black print, and trim to 2½" x 2½". Make 280 half-square-triangle units.

Make 280.

2 Sew four half-square-triangle units together as shown. Press seam allowances as indicated. Make 68.

Make 68.

3 Sew two half-square-triangle units, one black 2½" square, and one light 2½" square together into a four-patch unit. Press seam allowances as indicated. Make four.

Make 4.

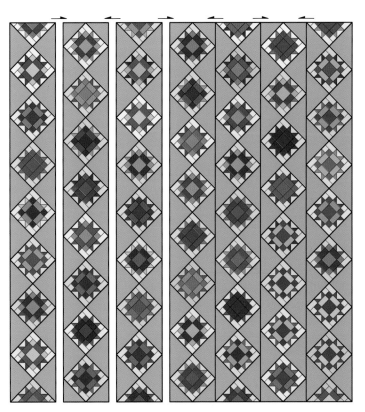

Quilt assembly

4 Sew 18 of the units from step 2 together for a side border. Press seam allowances in one direction. Make two. Sew 16 of the units from step 2 together with two of the units from step 3. Press. Make two for the top and bottom borders.

Make 2 of each.

Adding the Borders

After completing the center of the quilt, always measure the length and width before cutting borders. Refer to "Measuring for Borders" on page 93.

1 Sew the black 2¾" x 68½" strips to the sides of the quilt center. Press the seam allowances toward the border strips, and then add the black 2½" x 64½" strips to the top and bottom. Press.

2 Sew the pieced borders without corner units to the sides of the quilt top and press the seam allowances toward the inner border. Add the top and bottom pieced borders. Press.

3 Sew the black 7" x 80½" strips to the sides of the quilt top. Press seam allowances toward the outer border. Add the black 7" x 85½" strips to the top and bottom. Press.

Finishing the Quilt

1 Layer the quilt top with the batting and backing. Quilt by hand or machine. The featured quilt was machine quilted with zigzagging feathers in the cheddar background and pieced border, ditch quilting on the blocks, and a pumpkin seed motif on the outer border.

2 Add binding using the 1⅞"-wide strips. If you need additional details, go to ShopMartingale.com for free downloadable information.

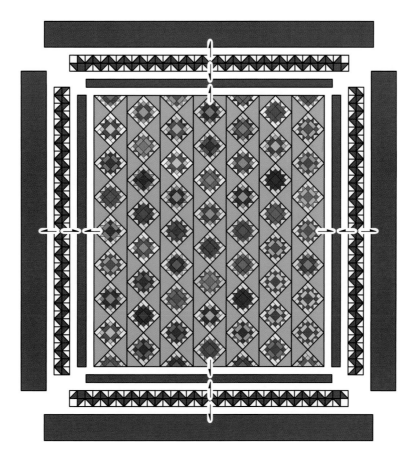

Adding borders

Antique Star

The most famous family of the Civil War, the "Fighting McCooks" of Carrollton, Ohio, was the largest immediate family to serve in the Union army. Three brothers—Daniel, John, and George—and their 14 sons served on 46 battlefields. Virtually no major battle in the western theater occurred without the presence of at least one of the Fighting McCooks.

They were as diverse as any large family, with doctors, lawyers, and businessmen among them, and nearly all were college educated. But the McCooks were united by one common element—their determination to preserve the Union. Their military roles included three major generals, three brigadier generals, one naval lieutenant, four surgeons, two colonels, one major, one lieutenant, one private (young Charles who enlisted at 17 and declined the lieutenant's commission he was offered), and one chaplain. Four of the Fighting McCooks lost their lives.

The McCook House, home of Major Daniel McCook, is located in Carrollton and is preserved as a memorial to Ohio's famous family. Charles and Barbara Whalen's book *The Fighting McCooks: America's Famous Fighting Family* (Westmoreland Press, 2006) follows the McCooks through the war and tells of the political, military, and social climate of the time. In this quilt, we've paid tribute to the McCook family by using the Ohio Star block.

1871 oil painting of the McCooks by Charles T. Webber

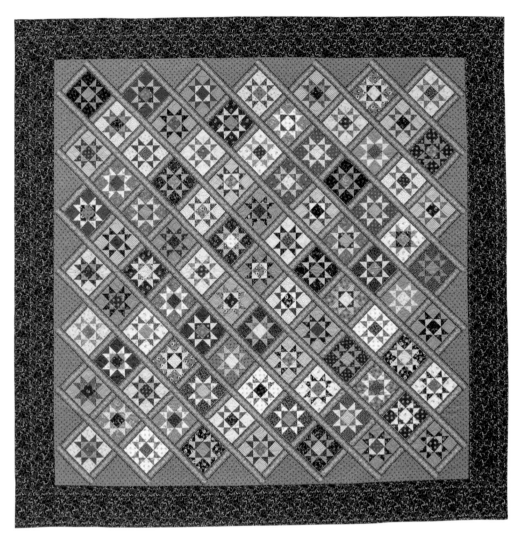

FINISHED QUILT: 91" x 91" ✳ FINISHED BLOCK: 6" x 6"
"Antique Star," designed by Paula Barnes, pieced by Mary Ellen Robison,
and machine quilted by Sharon Dixon

Materials

Yardage is based on 42"-wide fabric.

3¼ yards of medium-scale stripe for sashing

2¾ yards of black print for border

1 yard of green print for setting triangles

⅜ yard *each* of 11 assorted light prints for blocks

¼ yard *each* of 22 assorted medium to dark prints
for blocks

1 yard of dark print for binding

8½ yards of fabric for backing

99" x 99" piece of batting

Cutting

*Do not cut the lengthwise border strips from the black
print until the quilt center is complete and you have
determined the final measurements.*

From *each* of the 11 assorted light prints, cut:
    20 squares, 2½" x 2½" (220 total; 5 are extra)
    16 squares, 3½" x 3½" (176 total; 4 are extra)
**From *each* of the 22 assorted medium to dark
    prints, cut:**
    10 squares, 2½" x 2½" (220 total; 5 are extra)
    8 squares, 3½" x 3½" (176 total; 4 are extra)

From the medium-scale stripe, cut on the
  lengthwise **grain:**
  2 strips, 2" x 99½"
  2 strips, 2" x 84½"
  2 strips, 2" x 69½"
  2 strips, 2" x 54½"
  2 strips, 2" x 39½"
  2 strips, 2" x 24½"
  2 strips, 2" x 9½"
  98 rectangles, 2" x 6½"
From the green print, cut:
  6 squares, 11⅞" x 11⅞"; cut into quarters
    diagonally to make 24 triangles
  2 squares, 6¼" x 6¼"; cut in half diagonally to
    make 4 triangles
From the black print, cut on the *lengthwise* grain:
  2 strips, 7½" x 77"
  2 strips, 7½" x 91"
From the dark binding fabric, cut:
  10 strips, 1⅞" x 42", or bias strips to total 420"

Making the Blocks

1 Select two light 3½" squares. These can be the same or different, whichever you prefer. With a pencil, draw two diagonal lines on the wrong side of each, making an X.

2 Select two matching medium or dark 3½" squares and place a marked square on each, right sides together. Sew ¼" from each side of *one* of the pencil lines. Cut apart on the drawn lines and press the seam allowances toward the darker print.

Mark. Sew.

Cut. Press.

3 Sew the units together in pairs to make four hourglass units. (Note that the illustrations show two different lights. Make some blocks with the same light print to add variety and create an

antique look. The dark triangles will create the star points.) Trim and square up the hourglass units to 2½" x 2½", referring to "Trimming Hourglass Units" on page 58.

2½"
2½"

Make 4.

4 Select four matching light 2½" squares; these should match one of the lights in the hourglass units. Select a medium or dark 2½" square for the block center. This should be a different dark print than used in the hourglass units. (For variety, however, you may make some blocks with the same dark print.) Arrange the squares and the four hourglass units in three rows as shown. Sew the units into rows and press seam allowances toward the unpieced squares. Sew the rows together and press the seam allowances away from the center row.

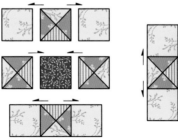 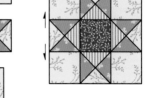

5 Repeat steps 1–4 to make 43 blocks with light backgrounds.

6 Repeat steps 1–3 to make hourglass units with two different or matching medium or dark 3½" squares. Use two matching light 3½" squares. These will be the star points in the blocks with dark backgrounds. Repeat step 4, selecting four dark 2½" squares and one light 2½" square. Make 43 blocks with dark backgrounds. You'll have one extra block to play with when laying out the quilt.

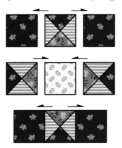 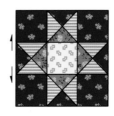

Constructing the Quilt

After completing the center of the quilt, always measure the length and width before cutting borders. Refer to "Measuring for Borders" on page 93.

1 Lay out the blocks in an on-point setting, with seven blocks across and seven blocks down. Rearrange until you are pleased with the color placement. Add the sashing pieces to the layout.

2 Sew the blocks and sashing rectangles together in rows as indicated in the quilt assembly diagram on page 59. Press the seam allowances toward the sashing. Place the block rows back in the layout.

3 Sew the block rows and sashing rows together and press seam allowances toward the sashing strips. Add the green side setting triangles. Press the seam allowances toward the triangles.

Trimming Hourglass Units

Making hourglass blocks or units slightly oversized allows you to trim them after sewing to the exact size needed, guaranteeing accuracy.

1 Place a square ruler on top of the block, lining up the diagonal line of the ruler with the diagonal line of the block. Divide the desired trimmed size of the block by two and make sure those lines of the ruler meet at the center of the block. For a 2½" unfinished Hourglass block, place the 1¼" lines at the block center. Make sure the 2½" lines of the ruler align with the opposite diagonal seam of the Hourglass block.

2 Trim the block along the top and right edges of the square ruler.

3 Rotate the block so that the newly trimmed sides align with the 2½" lines of the ruler. Align the diagonal line of the ruler with the diagonal seam of the block and make sure the 1¼" lines meet at the block center as in step 1.

4 Trim the block along the top and right edges of the ruler. You now have a perfect Hourglass block.

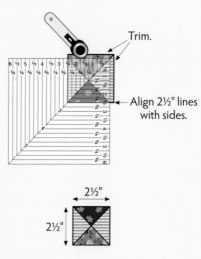

Trim.

Align 2½" lines with sides.

2½"

2½"

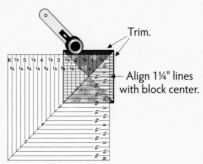

Trim.

Align 1¼" lines with block center.

4 Sew the rows together and press seam allowances in one direction. Add the four corner setting triangles last.

5 Attach the black 7½" x 77" strips to the sides of the quilt top, and press the seam allowances toward the border. Add the black 7½" x 91" strips to the top and bottom. Press.

Finishing the Quilt

1 Layer the quilt top with the batting and backing. Quilt by hand or machine. To contrast the intricate geometric lines of the design, the featured quilt was machine quilted with an allover feather design.

2 Add binding using the 1⅞"-wide strips. If you need additional details, go to ShopMartingale.com for free downloadable information.

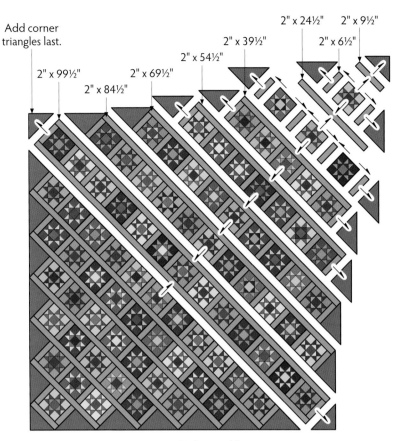

Add corner triangles last.

2" x 99½"
2" x 84½"
2" x 69½"
2" x 54½"
2" x 39½"
2" x 24½"
2" x 9½"
2" x 6½"

Quilt assembly

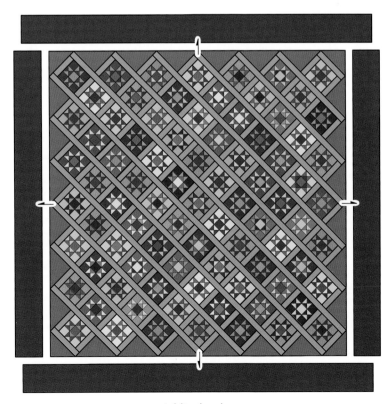

Adding borders

Wheatland

Wheatland, also known as the James Buchanan House, is a Federal-style brick house located in Lancaster Township, Lancaster County, Pennsylvania. Built in 1828, it was purchased in 1848 by James Buchanan, who would become the 15th president of the United States. It was his residence for nearly two decades.

James Buchanan was born on April 23, 1791, in a log cabin in Cove Gap, Pennsylvania. His family moved to Mercersburg, where he attended Old Stone Academy and later Dickinson College in Carlisle. He was nearly expelled for poor behavior, but after pleading for a second chance, he did graduate with honors. He later moved to Lancaster to practice law and was admitted to the bar in 1812.

Prior to his nomination for the presidency in 1856, Buchanan held many political offices: member of the House of Representatives, minister to Russia, US senator, secretary of state under President James Polk, and minister to Great Britain under President Franklin Pierce. Buchanan conducted his presidential campaign from Wheatland as a "front-porch campaign." He swept the Southern states, and many thought his tactic of circulating lithographs of Wheatland depicting it as a Northern "plantation estate" convinced the Southerners of his support.

Wheatland, the former home of John Buchanan

Buchanan was elected and served from 1857 to 1861. His inability or unwillingness to prevent secession and his refusal to take a stance for or against slavery have led many historians to rank his presidency as one of the worst in US history. He announced in his inaugural speech that he would not seek a second term, and he followed through on his promise. Buchanan retired in 1861 to his home, and died there at Wheatland seven years later.

FINISHED QUILT: 82" x 90½" ✳ **FINISHED BLOCK:** 6" x 6"
"Wheatland," designed by Paula Barnes, pieced by Mary Ellen Robison,
and machine quilted by Sharon Dixon

Materials

Yardage is based on 42"-wide fabric.

3¾ yards of navy print for pieced setting blocks,
   setting triangles, and fourth border
1½ yards of cheddar print #1 for blocks
1⅓ yards of light-tan print for pieced setting blocks
   and triangles
⅔ yard of cheddar print #2 for first and third borders
⅝ yard of medium-brown print for second border
¼ yard *each* of 8 assorted light prints for blocks
⅛ yard *each* of 28 assorted dark prints for blocks
1 yard of fabric for binding
7½ yards of fabric for backing
90" x 99" piece of batting

Cutting

*Do not cut the lengthwise border strips from the
navy-blue print until the quilt center is complete and
you have determined the final measurements.*

From *each* of the 28 assorted dark prints, cut:
   6 rectangles, 1½" x 7"
From *each* of the 8 assorted light prints, cut:
   3 strips, 1½" x 42"; crosscut into 14 rectangles,
      1½" x 7"
From cheddar print #1, cut:
   6 strips, 4½" x 42"; crosscut into 28 rectangles,
      4½" x 7"
   14 strips, 1½" x 42"; crosscut into 112 rectangles,
      1½" x 4½"

From the light-tan print, cut:

5 strips, 7" x 42"; crosscut into 21 squares, 7" x 7"

1 strip, 5⅛" x 42"; crosscut into 6 squares, 5⅛" x 5⅛". Cut in half diagonally to make 12 triangles.

From the navy print, cut:

4 strips, 7" x 42"; crosscut into 20 squares, 7" x 7"*

1 strip, 9¾" x 42"; crosscut into 4 squares, 9¾" x 9¾". Cut into quarters diagonally to make 16 triangles (2 are extra).

From the *remainder* of the navy print, cut on the *lengthwise* grain:

2 strips, 7½" x 76¼"

2 strips, 7½" x 82"

1 square, 7" x 7"*

8 squares, 5⅛" x 5⅛"; cut in half diagonally to make 16 triangles

From the medium-brown print, cut:

7 strips, 2½" x 42"

From cheddar print #2, cut:

14 strips, 1½" x 42"

From the binding fabric, cut:

10 strips, 1⅞" x 42", or bias strips to total 380"

You'll need a total of 21 squares. If you can cut them from the 4 strips, you won't need to cut the additional square.

Making the Checkerboard Blocks

We love how dynamic this simple block looks when paired with a large half-square-triangle unit as an alternate block.

1 Sew two matching dark 1½" x 7" rectangles and one 4½" x 7" rectangle of cheddar print #1 together. Press seam allowances toward the cheddar print and cut four segments, 1½" wide. Make 28 strip sets and cut a total of 112 segments.

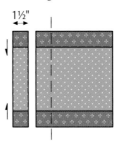

1½"

Make 28 strip sets.
Cut 112 segments.

2 Sew two matching dark 1½" x 7" rectangles and two matching light 1½" x 7" rectangles together. Press seam allowances toward the dark print and cut four segments, 1½" wide.

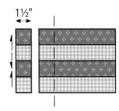

1½"

Cut 4 segments.

3 Sew the four segments together and press seam allowances in one direction.

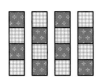

4 Repeat steps 2 and 3 to make a total of 56 checkerboard block units.

5 Sew 1½" x 4½" rectangles of cheddar print #1 to opposite sides of a checkerboard block unit. Press seam allowances toward the rectangles. Add matching segments from step 1 to the top and bottom; press. Make a total of 56 blocks.

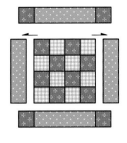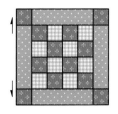

Make 56.

Making the Alternate Blocks

Referring to "Half-Square-Triangle Units" on page 91, mark the light-tan 7" squares and layer them right sides together with the navy 7" squares. Sew, cut, press seam allowances toward the navy print, and trim to 6½" x 6½". Make 42 half-square-triangle units.

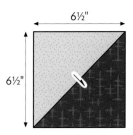

Make 42.

Making the Pieced Setting Triangles

Sew a light-tan 5⅛" triangle together with a navy 5⅛" triangle as shown. Press seam allowances toward the navy print. Make six of each as shown.

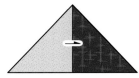

Make 6 of each.

Constructing the Quilt

After completing the center of the quilt, always measure the length and width before cutting borders. Refer to "Measuring for Borders" on page 93.

1 Lay out the blocks in an on-point setting, with seven blocks across and eight blocks down. Add the setting blocks and triangles to the layout, referring to the quilt assembly diagram for correct orientation. Rearrange the checkerboard blocks until you are pleased with the color placement.

2 Sew the blocks together into diagonal rows. Press seam allowances toward the setting blocks and triangles in each row. Place the block rows back in your quilt layout.

3 Sew the rows together. Add the corner triangles last. Press the seam allowances away from the center row.

Quilt assembly

4 For the first border, trim the selvages from the 1½" x 42" strips of cheddar print #2 and sew the strips together end to end. Press the seam allowances to one side. From this strip cut two strips, 68⅜" long, for the side borders and two strips, 62" long, for the top and bottom borders. Attach the side borders first, press the seam allowances toward the border strips, and then add the top and bottom borders. Press. Set aside the remainder of the pieced strip for the third border.

5 For the second border, trim the selvages from the brown 2½" x 42" strips and sew the strips together end to end. Press the seam allowances to one side. From this strip cut two strips, 70¼" long, for the side borders and two strips, 66" long, for the top and bottom borders. Attach the side borders first, press the seam allowances toward the brown strips, and then add the top and bottom borders. Press.

6 For the third border, cut the remaining pieced cheddar strip into two strips, 74¼" long, for the side borders and two strips, 68" long, for the top and bottom borders. Attach the side borders first, press the seam allowances toward the cheddar strips, and then add the top and bottom borders. Press.

7 Attach the navy 7½" x 76¼" strips to the sides of the quilt top, press the seam allowances toward the navy border, and then add the navy 7½" x 82" strips. Press.

Finishing the Quilt

1 Layer the quilt top with the batting and backing. Quilt by hand or machine. To contrast the straight lines and small elements of the design, the featured quilt was machine quilted with a large allover feather design.

2 Add binding using the 1⅞"-wide strips. If you need additional details, go to ShopMartingale.com for free downloadable information.

Adding borders

Crossroads

Shelby Foote is the Mississippi-born author of *The Civil War: A Narrative* (Random House: 1958, 1963, 1974), considered by many to be the definitive work on the Civil War. What started as a publisher's proposal for a short account of the Civil War was turned into an epic three-volume life's work. Over the span of 20 years, Foote wrote 500 to 600 words a day to create one of the most comprehensive accounts of what he described as our great national tragedy, the American Civil War.

Foote is quoted at the end of the third and last volume: "By way of possible extenuation, in response to complaints that it took me longer to write the war than the participant to fight it, I would point out that there were a good many more of them than there was of me."

In Ken Burns's PBS documentary *The Civil War*, 40 million viewers were drawn to Foote's melodious Southern drawl in his appearance as an expert on the war. The series aired on five consecutive nights in September 1990 and became the most-watched PBS special of all time, propelling Shelby Foote into the limelight overnight.

In the series, Foote describes the importance of studying the Civil War. "And it is very necessary if you're going to understand the American character in the 20th century, to learn about this enormous catastrophe in the mid-19th century. It was the crossroads of our being and it was a hell of a crossroads."

Three Confederate soldiers taken prisoner after the Battle of Gettysburg

FINISHED QUILT: 68½" x 85½" ✳ FINISHED BLOCK: 10½" x 10½"
"Crossroads," designed by Paula Barnes, pieced by Mary Ellen Robison,
and machine quilted by Cathy Peters and Lynn Graham

Materials

Yardage is based on 42"-wide fabric.

2⅝ yards of red border print for outer border

2⅜ yards of light print for blocks and sashing

1⅓ yards of black print for blocks, cornerstones, and
   inner border

1¼ yards of red print for setting triangles

10" x 12" piece *each* of 18 assorted dark prints
   for blocks

1 yard of black solid for binding

5¼ yards of fabric for backing

75" x 92" piece of batting

Cutting

From *each* of the 18 assorted dark prints, cut:
   4 squares, 2" x 2"
   8 rectangles, 2" x 3½"

From the light print, cut:
   39 strips, 2" x 42"; crosscut *28* of the strips into:
      234 squares, 2" x 2"
      48 strips, 2" x 11"

From the black print, cut:
   20 strips, 2" x 42"; crosscut *2* of the strips into
      31 squares, 2" x 2"

From the red print, cut:
   3 squares, 18¼" x 18¼"; cut into quarters
      diagonally to make 12 triangles (2 are extra)
   2 squares, 10½" x 10½"; cut in half diagonally to
      make 4 triangles
From the red border print, cut on the
   lengthwise **grain:**
   2 strips, 6½" x 90"
   2 strips, 6½" x 73"
From the black solid, cut:
   8 strips, 1⅞" x 42", or bias strips to total 320"

Making the Blocks

1 Sew a black-print and a light-print 2" x 42" strip together along the long edges. Press the seam allowances toward the black print. Make 11 strip sets and cut a total of 216 segments, 2" wide.

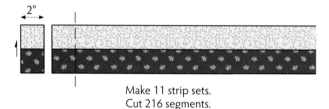

Make 11 strip sets.
Cut 216 segments.

2 Sew two segments from step 1 together to make a four-patch unit. Press seam allowances to one side. Make 72.

Make 72.

3 Sew four matching dark 2" squares and five light 2" squares together in three rows as shown. Press seam allowances as indicated by the arrows. Sew the rows together to make a nine-patch unit. Press.

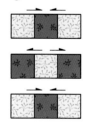

4 Using a pencil, draw a line diagonally from corner to corner on the wrong side of eight light 2" squares.

5 Place a marked square right sides together on one end of a dark 2" x 3½" rectangle that matches the squares in the nine-patch unit. Sew on the marked line. Trim ¼" from the line and press the seam allowances toward the light print. Repeat with a second rectangle, sewing in the opposite direction. Make four of each.

Make 4.

Make 4.

6 Sew two of the units from step 5 together with a strip-set segment from step 1. Press seam allowances away from the strip-set segment. Make four.

Make 4.

7 Arrange four of the four-patch units from step 2, the units from step 6, and the nine-patch unit in three rows as shown. Sew the units into rows. Press seam allowances as indicated by the arrows. Sew the rows together and press.

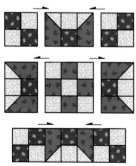 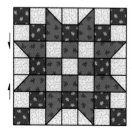

8 Repeat steps 3–7 to make 18 blocks.

Constructing the Quilt

After completing the center of the quilt, always measure the length and width before cutting borders. Refer to "Measuring for Borders" on page 93.

1 Lay out the blocks in an on-point setting with three blocks across and four blocks down. Add the sashing, cornerstones, and setting triangles to the layout. Rearrange the blocks until you are pleased with the color placement.

2 Sew the blocks and sashing together into rows as indicated in the quilt assembly diagram. Sew the sashing and cornerstones into rows. Press the seam allowances as indicated by the arrows. Sew a sashing row to a block row and add the setting triangles to the ends. Place the block rows back in the quilt layout.

Add corner triangles last.

Quilt assembly

3 Sew the rows together and press seam allowances toward the sashing. Add the corner triangles last and press toward the triangles.

4 For the inner border, trim the selvages from the black-print 2" x 42" strips and sew the strips together end to end. Press the seam allowances to one side. From this strip cut two strips, 70½" long, for the side borders and two strips, 56½" long, for the top and bottom borders. Attach the side borders first, press the seam allowances toward the border strips, and then add the top and bottom borders. Press.

5 Referring to "Mitered Borders" on page 91, add the border-print strips to all four sides of the quilt and miter the corners. Press.

Finishing the Quilt

1 Layer the quilt top with the batting and backing. Quilt by hand or machine. The featured quilt was machine quilted with a floral motif centered in each block and complementary floral designs in the setting triangles and border.

2 Add binding using the 1⅞"-wide strips. If you need additional details, go to ShopMartingale.com for free downloadable information.

Adding borders

Sallie's Quilt

arved at the base of the monument for the 11th Pennsylvania Infantry, situated on Oak Ridge in Gettysburg National Military Park, lies a Staffordshire bull terrier named Sallie. Given to Lieutenant William Terry as a pup, Sallie grew up with the regiment and became its loyal and beloved mascot.

Sallie's first battle was at Cedar Mountain in 1862. She remained with the colors throughout that conflict and many more after—Antietam, Fredericksburg, and Chancellorsville. She frequently positioned herself at the end of the battle line, barking ferociously at the enemy.

On the first day of fighting at Gettysburg, the 11th Pennsylvania was driven back from Oak Ridge; amid the confusion, Sallie went missing. Days later, she was discovered lying with the dead and wounded soldiers from that first day of battle. Although weak from lack of food and water, she recovered under the care of her soldiers and was able to return to the battlefield with them. Later that year at Spotsylvania, Sallie was wounded, but proudly bore her scar as a "red badge of courage."

On February 6, 1865, the 11th Pennsylvania, with Sallie by their side, attacked the Confederate lines at Hatcher's Run in Virginia. Sallie was shot and killed instantly. The men of the 11th buried Sallie where she lay on the battlefield.

In 1890, the remaining members of the 11th Pennsylvania Infantry dedicated a monument on Oak Ridge—a vigilant bronze soldier atop the pedestal and, at the base, brave and faithful Sallie.

The monument on Oak Ridge

FINISHED QUILT: 91¾" x 106¾" ✴ FINISHED BLOCK: 9" x 9"
"Sallie's Quilt," designed by Paula Barnes, pieced by Mary Ellen Robison,
and machine quilted by Marcella Pickett and Margie Love of Crooked Creek Quilts

Materials

Yardage is based on 42"-wide fabric.

5 yards of blue print for Chain blocks, setting triangles, and outer border

2⅓ yards of black print or solid for sashing and inner border

1 yard of cream print for Chain blocks and sashing squares

¼ yard *each* of 16 assorted cream reproduction prints or shirtings for Star blocks

¼ yard *each* of 16 assorted dark prints for Star blocks

5" x 10" piece *each* of 16 assorted medium prints for Star blocks

1 yard of fabric for binding

9 yards of fabric for backing

100" x 115" piece of batting

3" finished "Star Singles" papers* (optional)

*See "Using Star Singles" on page 75 before cutting fabrics.

Cutting

Do not cut the lengthwise border strips from the blue print until the quilt center is complete and you have determined the final measurements.

From *each* of the 16 cream prints or shirtings, cut:
   2 squares, 4½" x 4½"
   4 squares, 4¼" x 4¼"*

*See "Using Star Singles" on page 75 before cutting fabrics.

From *each* of the 16 medium prints, cut:
  2 squares, 4½" x 4½"

From *each* of the 16 dark prints, cut:
  4 squares, 4½" x 4½"
  4 squares, 4¼" x 4¼"*
  2 squares, 3½" x 3½"

From the cream print for blocks and sashing, cut:
  12 strips, 2" x 42"; crosscut *4* of the strips into
    71 squares, 2" x 2"
  2 strips, 3½" x 42"; crosscut into 18 squares,
    3½" x 3½"

From the blue print, cut:
  8 strips, 2" x 42"
  5 squares, 16⅛" x 16⅛"; cut into quarters
    diagonally to make 20 triangles (2 are extra)

**From the *remainder* of the blue print, cut on the
lengthwise grain:**
  2 strips, 6½" x 94¾"
  2 strips, 6½" x 91¾"
  2 squares, 9⅜" x 9⅜"; cut in half diagonally to
    make 4 triangles
  72 squares, 3½" x 3½"

From the black print, cut:
  6 strips, 9½" x 42"; crosscut into 120 rectangles,
    2" x 9½"
  9 strips, 2" x 42"

From the binding fabric, cut:
  11 strips, 1⅞" x 42", or 1⅞"-wide bias strips to
    total 420"

*See "Using Star Singles" below before cutting fabrics..

Using Star Singles

If you use the 3" Star Singles papers, do not cut the 4¼" squares. Instead, cut the following pieces.

From *each* of the 16 assorted cream prints and 16 assorted dark prints, cut:
  1 square, 8½" x 8½"

Making the Star Blocks

For each Star block, you'll need a cream print or shirting, a medium print, and two dark prints in the following sizes.

- **Cream print or shirting:** 1 square, 4½" x 4½", and 2 squares, 4¼" x 4¼"
- **Medium print:** 1 square, 4½" x 4½"
- **Dark print #1:** 2 squares, 4½" x 4½", and 2 squares, 4¼" x 4¼"
- **Dark print #2:** 1 square, 3½" x 3½"

1 With a pencil or fabric marker, draw two diagonal lines from corner to corner on the wrong side of the cream and medium-print 4½" squares, making an X.

Mark.

2 With right sides together, place the marked cream square on a 4½" square of dark print #1. Sew ¼" from each side of *one* of the pencil lines. Cut on both pencil lines and press seam allowances toward the darker fabric.

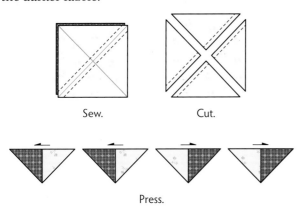

3 Repeat step 2 with the marked medium-print square and a 4½" square of dark print #1.

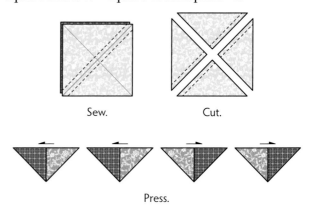

4 Join the units from steps 2 and 3 to make four hourglass units. Follow the steps in "Trimming Hourglass Units" on page 58, placing the 1¾" lines of the ruler at the center of the unit; square up the hourglass units to 3½" x 3½".

Make 4.

5 Referring to "Half-Square-Triangle Units" on page 91, mark the two cream or shirting 4¼" squares and layer them right sides together with the 4¼" squares of dark print #1. Sew, cut, press seam allowances toward the dark print, and trim to 3½" x 3½". Make four half-square-triangle units.

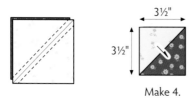

Make 4.

6 Arrange the four half-square-triangle units, the four hourglass units, and the 3½" square of dark print #2 in rows as shown. Sew the units into rows and press as indicated by the arrows. Sew the rows together and press.

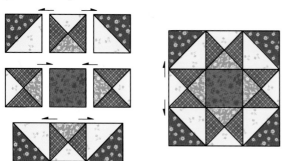

7 Repeat steps 1–6 to make 32 Star blocks.

Making the Chain Blocks

1 Sew a cream 2" x 42" strip to a blue 2" x 42" strip along the long edges to make a strip set. Press seam allowances toward the blue strip. Make eight strip sets. Cut the strip sets into 144 segments, 2" wide.

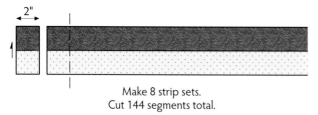

Make 8 strip sets.
Cut 144 segments total.

2 Sew two segments together to make a four-patch unit. Make 72.

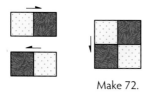

Make 72.

3 Arrange four of the four-patch units, four blue 3½" squares, and one cream 3½" square together in three rows. Sew the units into rows and press as indicated by the arrows. Sew the rows together and press. Make 18 Chain blocks.

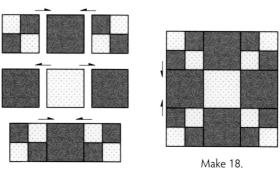

Make 18.

Constructing the Quilt

After completing the center of the quilt, always measure the length and width before cutting borders. Refer to "Measuring for Borders" on page 93.

1 Lay out the Chain blocks and the Star blocks in an on-point setting, referring to the quilt assembly diagram on page 78. Add the cream 2" cornerstone squares and the black 2" x 9½" sashing rectangles to the layout. Rearrange the Star blocks until you are pleased with the color placement.

2 Sew the block rows and sashing rows together as indicated in the quilt assembly diagram. Press seam allowances toward the sashing rectangles. Sew the sashing rows and block rows together in pairs and add the side setting triangles. Press the seam allowances toward the setting triangles. Place the rows back in the quilt layout.

3 Sew the rows together and add the corner triangles last. Press toward the triangles.

4 For the inner border, trim the selvages from the black 2" x 42" strips and sew the strips together end to end. Press the seam allowances to one side. From this strip cut two strips, 91¾" long, for the side borders and two strips, 79¾" long, for the top and bottom borders. Attach the side borders first, press the seam allowances toward the border strips, and then add the top and bottom borders.

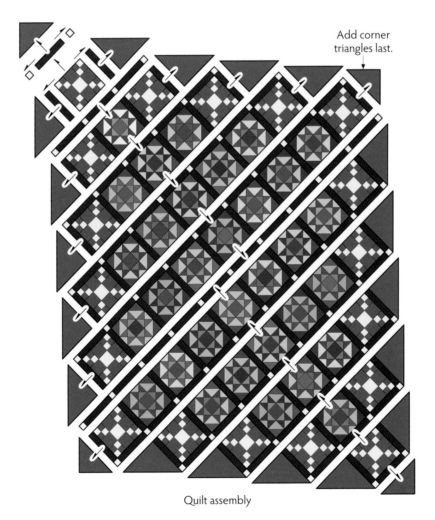

Add corner triangles last.

Quilt assembly

5 Attach the blue 6½" x 94¾" strips to the sides of the quilt top. Press the seam allowances toward the blue border. Add the blue 6½" x 91¾" strips to the top and bottom. Press.

Finishing the Quilt

1 Layer the quilt top with the batting and backing. Quilt by hand or machine. The featured quilt was machine quilted with curved diamonds in the Chain blocks and double outline stitching in the Star blocks to emphasize the shapes in the blocks. Pumpkin seed and diamond designs were stitched on the inner border, and feathers were quilted on the outer border.

2 Add binding using the 1⅞"-wide strips. If you need additional details, go to ShopMartingale.com for free downloadable information.

Adding borders

Oak Alley

Oak Alley Plantation is a historic plantation on the Mississippi River in Vacherie, Louisiana. The beautiful Southern mansion was built in 1839 by Jacques Roman, but it is the quarter-mile-long alley of 28 majestic oaks forming a canopy or alley between the house and the Mississippi River that it is most known for. The double rows of live oaks were planted in the early eighteenth century, long before the mansion was in existence.

Originally established as a sugar cane plantation, Oak Alley eventually became a cattle ranch when it was purchased by Andrew and Josephine Stewart in the 1920s. When Josephine Stewart died in 1972, the house and grounds became the property of the Oak Alley Foundation and it was opened to the public. In 2013, the Foundation opened "Slavery at Oak Alley," a permanent educational exhibit covering the history of slavery at Oak Alley from the 1800s through emancipation.

Oak Alley is probably the most photographed and recognizable plantation and has been the setting for numerous motion pictures and TV shows: *"Interview with a Vampire," "Primary Colors,"* and *"Hush . . . Hush Sweet Charlotte,"* and the daytime soap operas *"Days of Our Lives"* and *"The Young and the Restless."*

This pattern was inspired by the iconic Oak Alley Plantation.

FINISHED QUILT: 78½" x 78½" ✳ **FINISHED BLOCK:** 10½" x 10½"
"Oak Alley," designed by Paula Barnes, made by Mary Ellen Robison,
machine quilted by Marcella Pickett and Margie Love of Crooked Creek Quilts

Materials

2½ yards of border print for fourth border

2¼ yards of cream print for blocks, second border, and pieced third border

1½ yards of gold print for blocks and setting triangles

1 yard of tan print for sashing

⅔ yard of black print for pieced sashing and first border

¼ yard or 1 fat quarter *each* of 13 assorted dark prints for blocks, pieced sashing, and pieced third border

1 yard of fabric for binding

7¼ yards of fabric for backing

86" x 86" piece of batting

1½" finished "Star Singles" papers* (optional)

3" finished "Star Singles" papers* (optional)

See "Using Star Singles" on page 83.

Cutting

From *each* of the 13 assorted dark prints, cut:

    2 squares, 2" x 2"

    9 squares, 2¾" x 2¾"*

    4 squares, 4¼" x 4¼"*

    3 squares, 2⅜" x 2⅜"; cut in half diagonally to make 6 triangles

    1 square, 3½" x 3½"

    1 square, 2½" x 2½"

See "Using Star Singles" on page 83 before cutting fabrics.

the cream border. Add the pieced border strips with squares to the top and bottom and press.

9 Referring to "Mitered Borders" on page 91, add the border-print strips to all four sides of the quilt and miter the corners. Press.

Finishing the Quilt

1 Layer the quilt top with the batting and backing. Quilt by hand or machine. The featured quilt was machine quilted in keeping with the formal style of the design, including crosshatching in the trees, small feathers in the block background, twisted cables in the block sashing, and feathers in the setting triangles. The cream border has a leaf motif to emphasize the oak tree theme.

2 Add binding using the 1⅞"-wide strips. If you need additional details, go to ShopMartingale.com for free downloadable information.

Adding borders

QUILTMAKING BASICS

Quiltmaking is the result of fabrics, tools, and skills coming together in a wonderful combination. With the right fabrics, the proper tools, and basic sewing skills, anyone can make a quilt. The questions then become: "What are the right fabrics? What are the proper tools? And what skills are needed?" We hope to answer those questions here.

In addition, we've included specific instructions for techniques used in making the quilts in the book, such as constructing half-square-triangle units and adding mitered borders. For further assistance with any aspect of quiltmaking, we suggest that you take classes at your favorite quilt shop, check out some of the many excellent quilting books, and visit ShopMartingale.com/HowtoQuilt for free downloadable information about topics such as rotary cutting, assembling the quilt sandwich, binding, and more.

Fabric

How to choose the right fabrics? Hmmm, if you're like most quilters, you probably have more than enough fabric already, and most of it could even be considered "right." But do feel free to shop! (You know you want to!) All the quilts featured in this book were designed and pieced using 1800s reproduction fabrics. Fabrics reminiscent of that time period include plaids, checks, stripes, polka dots, and shirtings, in color palettes that encompass reds, blues, blacks, browns, madder reds and turkey reds, cheddars, bubblegum pinks, and poison greens. These are the prints and colors that we love and prefer to work with, but that shouldn't prevent you from piecing any of these quilts in fabrics that *you* consider to be right—perhaps batiks, or even a combination of fabric styles. These will be your quilts; experiment with your "right" fabrics.

Reproduction fabrics

Tools

The proper tools of the quiltmaking trade include rotary cutters, rulers, cutting mats, sharp scissors, all-cotton thread, and your favorite sewing machine in good working order (clean, oiled, and ready to go).

Rotary cutter and cutting mat: Always keep a sharp blade in your rotary cutter. It will help with accuracy and ensure that your fabric is cut smoothly. The cutting mat should be as large as you have space for.

Rulers: Our favorite size for cutting strips and borders is the 6½" x 24" ruler, but square rulers are very handy for squaring up blocks. The 6½" and 9½" square rulers are the sizes we use most often.

Thread: We prefer 100% cotton thread to blend with the cotton fabrics in our quilts.

Skills

We all come to quiltmaking with varying skill levels and experiences, but accuracy is probably the most important qualification needed to successfully complete a quilt. Let's start with accuracy in cutting.

The instructions for all the projects in this book involve rotary cutting, and a standard ¼"-wide seam allowance is included in all measurements. Before you begin cutting, we suggest pressing your fabric well and putting a new blade in your rotary cutter. These are basic steps that go a long way toward successful cutting.

An accurate ¼" seam allowance is also essential in quiltmaking. Consider purchasing a ¼" presser foot for your sewing machine. Whether you use a ¼" foot or a standard foot, take the time to test your accuracy before you begin piecing your project. To check accuracy, follow these steps.

1 Cut three 1½" x 4" strips.

2 Sew the strips together. Press the seam allowances toward the outer strips.

3 Using a ruler, measure the width of the center strip. It should measure 1". If your center strip is larger than 1", your seam allowance is too narrow. If your center strip is smaller than 1", your seam allowance is too wide. Cut new strips and repeat until the center strip measures exactly 1".

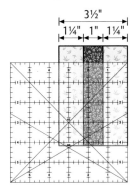

You can also use ¼" graph paper to check your seam allowance. Place a piece of the graph paper under the presser foot and sew on the first ¼" line. Affix a piece of painter's tape or ¼" quilter's tape along the edge of the paper. Sew three strips together using the seam guide and check the center strip for accuracy. Once you know it's in the correct position, build up the seam guide with another layer or two of tape.

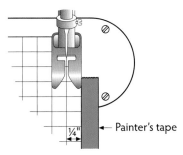

Painter's tape

After sewing seams accurately, pressing becomes the next important step. Recommended pressing directions for seam allowances are included throughout the project instructions. Remember, you are pressing to set seams, not ironing the wrinkles out of a man's dress shirt!

Half-Square-Triangle Units

We love half-square-triangle units, as you can see from our quilts! They add so much to a simple block. There are many different methods and tools available for making them, and you may already have a favorite technique. If so, feel free to use it. For these projects, we've generally used the technique of piecing the units from layered squares, without cutting triangles first.

We've also provided cutting options for some projects in which purchased triangle papers would be a good option. We like the Star Singles papers for ease and accuracy and often use them in our quiltmaking. They make several identical half-square-triangle units at a time. Star Singles papers were designed by Liz Eagen of Spinning Star Design. They are widely available at quilt shops and online.

When making half-square-triangle units without the papers, we cut squares oversized and trim the final units after pressing. This guarantees complete accuracy.

In the steps that follow, we've used 1" finished half-square-triangle units as an example.

1 Cut a light and a dark square, 1¼" larger than the desired finished size. In this case, cut the squares 2¼" x 2¼".

2 With a pencil or fabric marker and ruler, draw a diagonal line from corner to corner on the wrong side of the lighter 2¼" square.

3 Place the marked square on the dark 2¼" square with right sides together. Align the raw edges and sew ¼" from each side of the marked line.

Mark diagonal.
Sew ¼" away from
each side of the line.

4 Cut on the marked line. You'll have two identical half-square-triangle units. Press seam allowances toward the darker triangle.

Cut on
marked line.

Press.

5 Using a square ruler, trim and square up the units to 1½" x 1½", aligning the 45º line of your ruler with the seam. Make sure that the unit under the ruler extends beyond the 1½" marks and trim the right and top edges with your rotary cutter. Rotate the unit 180º, align the newly cut edges with the 1½" marks, and trim the right and top edges.

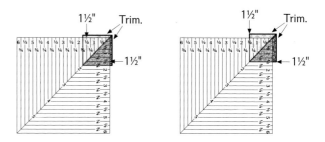

Mitered Borders

Once the blocks have been pieced together, it's time to add the borders to your quilt. There are many lovely border prints and stripes available, often with large floral motifs that just call out for mitering. Mitered borders require extra length, and we use a formula to determine the length of fabric needed. First measure the width and length of your quilt through the middle. Decide how wide you want the border to be, and then fill in the blanks.

$$\underline{\hspace{3cm}} + (2 \times \underline{\hspace{3cm}}) + 5"$$
Length (or width)   width of the border
of the quilt

Note that sometimes you may want to match a design at the corners. In these cases, cut the borders even longer to allow for matching the motifs before cutting the borders to the final length.

Follow the steps below to ensure a well-mitered border.

1 Center and pin a border strip to one side of the quilt top. Sew the border strip to the quilt top using a ¼" seam allowance, starting and stopping ¼" from the edge. Backstitch at the beginning and end to

secure the stitches. Press seam allowances toward the border strip.

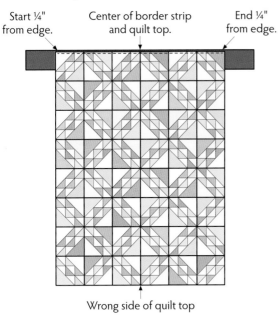

Start ¼" from edge. Center of border strip and quilt top. End ¼" from edge.

Wrong side of quilt top

2 Repeat step 1 for each side of the quilt.

3 Fold the quilt diagonally with right sides together; align the raw edges of two adjacent border strips. Pin the two borders together.

4 Place a long acrylic ruler along the folded edge of the quilt. Align the 45° line of the ruler with the border stitching line. With a pencil, draw a line from the point where the ¼" seamline begins to the raw edge of the border strip. Pin along this line to hold the two borders in place. Lift one border strip and check to see if the miter is correct.

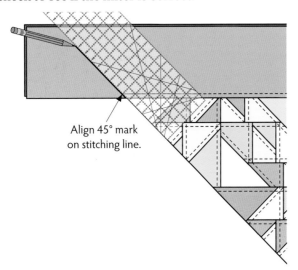

Align 45° mark on stitching line.

Draw a line from the seam intersection to outer edge of borders.

5 Beginning at the end of the border seam, sew along the pencil line to the edge of the borders. Open the borders to see if the seam lies flat and any design motifs line up. If the corner is sewn correctly, fold back on the diagonal again and trim, leaving a ¼" seam allowance. Press the seam allowances open.

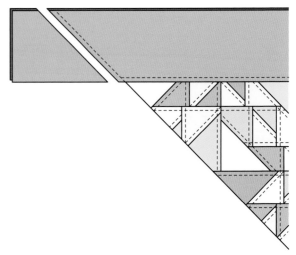

6 Repeat steps 3–5 for the remaining four corners.

A mitered border print adds the perfect final touch to "Oak Alley."

Measuring for Borders

Always measure your quilt before cutting borders. The cutting instructions for each of our projects indicates the lengths to cut, but this is based on a consistently accurate ¼" seam allowance and perfect piecing throughout the quilt top.

Measure the quilt from top to bottom through the center to find the length, and measure from side to side through the center to find the width.

Quilting

Your top is complete, so now it's time to prepare it for quilting. For many of us, that means making a backing and passing the project on to a machine quilter. The pattern instructions provide our yardage recommendations for a pieced backing. They allow for at least 4" to 6" extra on each side of the quilt, or a backing that is 8" to 12" larger than the finished quilt dimensions.

Binding

We most often use a double-fold straight-grain binding on our quilts, but we cut our strips 1⅞" wide, which is slightly narrower than what is often suggested. We find this width provides a nice tight binding and apparently is historically accurate for our reproduction quilts. Each project includes the number of binding strips to cut, and the yardage is enough to cut 2½"-wide strips if you prefer, either across the fabric width or on the bias.

We recently learned that binding cut on the lengthwise grain is not recommended. Crossgrain strips have more flexibility and stretch, ensuring that your quilt will lie flat when bound. Sew the strips end to end to make the continuous binding you will need.

Don't Forget a Label

Now that your quilt is finished, please remember to add a label. Some things to include, in addition to your full name, are the date you began the quilt, the date you completed it, your hometown, the name of the quilter (if not you), and the name of the recipient (if the quilt is a gift).

ABOUT THE AUTHORS

Paula Barnes (left) and Mary Ellen Robison (right) met more than 15 years ago when they both moved to the same street in Katy, Texas. Paula taught quilting classes at the local quilt shop and Mary Ellen was the devoted student. They quickly formed a friendship that went beyond their love of quilting and reproduction fabric to become Red Crinoline Quilts.

Although they met in Texas, each one comes from a different part of the country. Mary Ellen was born and raised in New York and Paula in Georgia—a true North/South friendship. Learning from her mom's expertise, Mary Ellen began sewing at the age of 12 and made most of her own clothes as she grew up. The year 1975 saw a resurgence in quilting due to the upcoming Bicentennial Celebration so Mary Ellen made her first quilt, a baby quilt that defied almost all of the rules of quiltmaking. Fortunately, shortly after that initial attempt, Mary Ellen took her first quilt class and the spell was cast. Being a wife, mother of three, full-time school librarian, and seamstress for her three children took most of her time, but her love of quilting and fabric was always present. Relocating to Texas, meeting Paula, and discovering reproduction fabrics reminded Mary Ellen of her passion.

Mary Ellen and her husband Peter now live in St. Petersburg, Florida, where she divides her time between sewing quilts, cruising, and traveling to see their three children: Megan in Louisville, Kentucky; Brett, daughter-in-law- Meredith, and granddaughters Sydney and Julianne in Ballston Lake, New York; and Caitlin in Tampa, Florida.

Paula began quilting in 1989 after moving to Dallas, Texas. Not knowing anyone, she decided to take her six-month old daughter to the Dallas Quilt Show. Three days later, she was hooked. After discovering that hand piecing wasn't her thing, Paula visited a notions counter and purchased the tools she would need to cut out and piece her quilt tops. Once she completed her fourth top, she was asked to teach a class at a local quilt store. Her husband JR encouraged her to give it a shot and the rest, as they say, is history. Paula taught in the Dallas/Fort Worth area for over 25 years, and in the past nine years has traveled and taught at various shops and quilt guilds throughout the United States.

Paula lives in the Houston area and is mom to three grown daughters: Ashley, Amy, Alison, son-in-law David, and grandmother (or MiMi) to granddaughter Sophie and grandson John.

Both Mary Ellen and Paula enjoyed other crafts and textile arts before discovering quilting. They still try to find the time to crochet, cross stitch, and smock, but it is quilting that has become their passion.

ACKNOWLEDGMENTS

We have all heard it takes a village to raise a child, but it would seem the same thing could be said for making a quilt. It's only through the help and support of many talented people that our quilts are able to appear in this book.

First and foremost, thank you to Karen Burns of Martingale for believing our quilts were "book worthy," and for convincing us that we should and could actually write a book. Thank you to the staff at Martingale for their help and assistance during this whole process.

And now to our quilt village. Once the quilt top is designed and pieced, it's out of our hands. We are very fortunate to have the help of multiple very talented quilters who are willing to accommodate our crazy schedule. A special thank-you to Marcella Pickett and Margie Love of Crooked Creek Quilts, Lynn Graham and Cathy Peters of Longarm Quilting Services, and Sharon Dixon of Katy T-Shirt Quilts for making our quilts look so beautiful with their outstanding quilting, and also for going the extra mile for us.

No quilt is complete until the binding is sewn on, and again we have dear friends who are willing to help us. Thank you to Gloria Parsons, Vicky Iannucci, and Shirley Chriss for your help.

In our rush to meet a deadline, we often ran out of time to piece just one more quilt and had to ask our friends for their assistance. "Civil War Generals" (page 22) was one of these quilts. Thank you to Robin Sutherlin for being there when we needed you.

And where would we be without our families? Thank you for your love and support throughout this journey. Your words of encouragement, your moments of listening, and of course your physical labor as you helped us set up our "store" at numerous quilt shows around the country were all appreciated.

Finally, thank you to our fans—the quilters who have supported us, bought our patterns and kits, and boosted our self-esteem!